PRAISE FOR THEO
AND
TAKE CARE OF DYING—GET

D0118004

Theo Wells has taken a topic that the majority of us want to ignore, deny, avoid, run away from and basically put off until we are "old" or as she makes very clear, until it is too late. From the very beginning of the book your attention is grabbed and your denial is left by the wayside, by her sense of humor, down to earth tone, personal stories and a healthy dose of warning us about the dangers of leaving your future health care and dying up to "others." Theo makes the process of aging, something over which we have no control, into a process where we have a lot of control over the quality of our aging and dying. The vignettes, practical advice, forms and a deep understanding of the laws and issues makes this book a wonderful and exceptional resource.

> —*Rachel Bulbulian, MSW, LICSW, Rochester, Minnesota*

In the very last sentence of **Take Care of Dying—Get On With Living,** author Theo Wells says of the information in the book, "I trust it works as well for you as it has for me." I have no doubts that it will, because this book is so expertly researched, so richly experienced, and so skillfully written.

With humor and with gritty determination to get her message out to those of us who are aging, to those of us who will die (ahem, in case you weren't aware, that's ALL of us!) . . . Theo does us the great favor of walking with us through the documentation and planning that will insure, as much as possible, that our wishes are honored in our final years and days.

The trick, of course, is that, just as we must actually CREATE those end-of-life documents and HAVE those all-important conversations with family, friends, and healthcare personnel, so we must actually READ this amazing book in order to partake of its wisdom.

The reading is a pleasure, the illustrative stories are rich, and the explanatory charts and graphs are spot on for clarity. READ this book—and give copies to your friends and family as well. Then "take care of dying" so you can "get on with living"!

> —*Cynthia Trenshaw, Professional Fiduciary, Guardian ad Litem, author of* Meeting in the Margins: An Invitation to Encounter Society's Invisible People

This book could not be a better gift to ourselves and those we love. Through stories and answers to specific questions, Theo brings light to a commonly avoided subject in an incisive and friendly way. Far from being a downer, Theo makes understanding the nuts and bolts of this unfamiliar territory a welcome friend.

> —*Connie Dawson, PhD, author of* Life Beyond Shame: Rewriting the Rules

This book makes an important contribution to a subject that many of us avoid as much as possible. In addition to being well researched and offering practical tools for making decisions about end-of-life choices, it also injects throughout a refreshing look at the author's personal experiences and decisions. Very helpful and very readable!

—*Miriam Sonn Raabe, RN, PhD, author of* Bite into the Day

Take Care of Dying—Get on with Living is a readable, even personable, guide for those seeking to find a way to manage their own transitions. More than this, it opened my eyes to the desirability of doing so. I now have a responsible and informed Agent who will manage the process for me, should I become unable to do so for myself. I have a Health Care Directive that will guide my Agent, the drafting of which helped me be much more specific about my values than would otherwise have been the case. I also have a draft durable power of attorney for health care which I have discussed with my legal advisor and will finalize in the near future. These efforts in turn led to my drafting a durable power of attorney for financial matters and to restructuring my last will and testament. Theo Wells' book not only stimulated me to get these matters "put to bed", so I can get on with living, but also provided me with a provocative and enjoyable reading experience.

—*Michael Moch, Professor Emeritus, Eli Broad Graduate School of Management, Michigan State University*

This book has it all: wisdom, wit, and a wealth of practical information. Every question or concern about end-of-life issues is addressed here in a way that is thought-provoking and motivating. Theo Wells has done a great service for those who have yet to make critical decisions about their wishes at life's end. Her experience, her passion, her clear writing, and her creative tools make this book a necessary resource.

—*Corrine Bayley, Director of the Center for Bioethics, Orange, California (retired)*

TAKE CARE OF

Dying

GET ON WITH

Living

End-of-Life Planning that Works

Theo Wells

PERMISSIONS STATEMENTS

MergerWatch–All versions of the Work that include the Selection shall contain the following statement: "Working to Protect Patients' Rights" is reprinted with kind permission from MergerWatch website: *www.mergerwatch.org.*

Unitarian Universalist Association–All versions of the Work that include the Selection shall contain the following statement: "The Right to Die with Dignity"; Unitarian Universalist Association 1988 Resolution appears with permission of the Unitarian Universalist Association.

DISCLAIMER

This book is designed to provide information related to end-of-life issues only. This information is provided and sold with the knowledge that this self-publishing author does not offer medical or legal advice. In case of need of such advice, consult with a physician or an elderlaw attorney. Every effort has been made to make the book as accurate and current as possible, but there may be errors or omissions. Therefore this book should serve only as a general guide and not as a complete and accurate source of subject information, and is intended only to inform and educate.

Abiding Nowhere Press
Greenbank, Washington 98253

Cynthia Trenshaw
Friend
My Durable Power of Attorney for Health Care

CONTENTS

PREFACE

This book had to be written. How can anyone puzzle through the many unanswerable questions that come up about a future we may not want to face?

My first problem was figuring out what the professionals were talking about. If I'm going to write an advance directive, some expert should tell me, in plain English, what that is. Sometimes there is a problem with plain English. For example, in an article about elder abuse, quoted in the well-respected New England Journal of Medicine, we find this: *Many initial attempts to define the clinical spectrum of the phenomenon and to formulate effective intervention strategies were limited by their anecdotal nature or were epidemiologically flawed.*[1] I'll take "their anecdotal nature" any day.

In this book I include many stories. Stories show what happens: you are inside the action. And stories let you empathize with the storyteller. They come alive; you walk in the shoes of another and share the experiences.

Or try this: what's an advance directive? Directing what? Advance—before what? Or is it advancing a particular idea? Is it one or two documents? Put the two words together and how would you know you're supposed to choose an agent/proxy and should make choices for future tough situations about your health care? Without initial caps, you may not even notice these words. Try this:

Advance Directive

Would that look more important? It's the only way I can think of to wave a red flag and holler: "Hey! This is important! Time to say what you do and don't want!"

I use initial caps several places just to call your attention to something important or different, like LST=Life Saving Treatments (which at times may mean prolonging life). So I learn a medical shorthand for decisions that are mine—and yours—to make.

We are engaged in a kind of language translation. For instance, I use digits instead of spelling out numbers. It's easier for me to calculate in my head this way. And I like an informal, conversational way of discussing these matters. Ordinary fear of death that many readers feel seems to melt away when we just talk with each other.

Searching for information online can be done easily by using simple reasoning. By doing your own searching, you are likely to run across information you didn't expect to find. Search engines are gifts to relative novices like me. I'm impressed with the growing amount of information that continues to come up as one snoops around. For years I've had a habit of writing in or underlining special books I own. I hope this book will be that kind for you, helping you think through different possibilities and feeling confident about making your own decisions. When all else fails, trust your gut.

"It is the fate of every human being," Oliver Sacks writes in *Gratitude,*

"to be a unique individual,
to find his own path,
to live his own life,
to die his own death."[2]

THE PUZZLE

One of the greatest gifts you can give your family is to tell them your end-of-life decisions and whom you choose to speak for you when needed. Eventually the person you choose to represent you may have to make your decisions for you. They will need to know the right answers—*your* answers. How are you going to do that? That's the puzzle:

> *How can you make decisions about unknown illnesses (that you don't think you'll get anyway) occurring in an unknown future, involving unknown treatments, with unknown effects on your body, mind and purse?*

Recent laws give you control over key decisions about which you may have strong feelings. Your personal values, family and friends are involved. You have the power to legally choose a Durable Power of Attorney for Health Care (your Agent) to speak for you if you can't speak for yourself. You also have the power to state your values as general guidelines for health decisions and to state specifically what you DO or DO NOT want done when hospitalized. You are not at the mercy of the gods unless you choose to be. Yet so far, only 25 to 30 percent of us are using these laws.

To me it didn't get personal until I had moved to another state and needed to change my Will. That's when I discovered the many ways to take care of my declining health while I'm alive. My ailing heart made me think. I was pushing eighty.

Early on I accidentally met the person who would become my Agent. She introduced me to the POLST (Physician Orders for Life-Sustaining Treatment) form, a document designed to inform the medical team—from paramedics to ER staff—of your expectations for treatment. One evening over dinner, she asked me this: "If you were in an accident and both your heart and breathing stopped, would you want to be resuscitated?" At the time, the only answer I could think of was, "Well, I suppose so. Then I could go to the hospital to find out whether or not I should have been resuscitated." You can see how well informed I was when I started this whole business.

Here's what happened next.

One day I found my way to a heart specialist who, after taking a flurry of pictures of my heart, concluded, "You're in good shape."

Aha! I thought, I'll ask him. "If I were in an accident and both my heart and breathing stopped, should I be resuscitated?"

"Absolutely not," he said. "At your age, your odds of any kind of a viable life afterward is less than 2 percent."

Wow! That got my attention. My mission became, "How do I get a DNR (Do Not Resuscitate) order and make it stick?" I didn't want any chance of becoming another Terri Schiavo, the landmark right-to-die case, where Terri lay in a comatose state for fifteen years before the courts let her off life support in 2005.

I've been researching end-of-life options ever since.

Most of us go through that strange process called aging. But many of us just don't get it until we are past sixty or sixty-five. We finally become conscious that our bodies are marching to a different drummer than our minds. Over the years you build up expectations of how your body works. And it usually does. Then one day it doesn't. It seems to have found a mind—an agenda—all its own. It doesn't have the courtesy to let you know, nor ask your advice. You can't control it. It controls you most of the time. Watch for warning signs and pay attention.

The good news is there are ways to stay in control of the uncontrollable. Since 1992 all states have laws that provide for Advance Directives (ADs) which are documents for giving directions to others before you get in serious health trouble. The two basic documents are:

- **Durable Power of Attorney for Health Care (DPOA-HC)** which empowers someone to speak for you—an Agent—if you become dysfunctional for a short time, or if you slip into a more permanent condition, such as a Persistent Vegetative State (PVS).

- **Health Care Directive (HCD),** a statement of your values and goals with specific instructions for your care, whether it's end-of-life decisions or a hospital trip.

Between 1976 and 1992 all fifty states adopted basic Natural Death Acts. These laws allow you to die naturally without Life-Sustaining Treatments if you so choose. Most states make special provisions for people who have become comatose but have left no word of what they want done in such a situation. Here's what the State of Washington provides, as written in its Code of Law:

> *The legislature finds that adult persons have the fundamental right to control the decisions relating to the rendering of their own health care, including the decision to have life-sustaining treatment withheld or withdrawn in instances of terminal condition or permanent unconscious condition....The legislature further finds that modern medical technology has made possible the artificial prolongation of human life beyond natural limits.....and that... such prolongation of the process of dying...may cause loss of patient dignity, and unnecessary pain and suffering, while providing nothing medically necessary or beneficial to the patient.*[1]

Search for your state's Natural Death Act and how it applies where you live.

Since you can't predict what future illnesses or accidents lie ahead, let's get creative. One way through the Puzzle is to use both sides of your brain to write your directives. Your right brain, creative and sensitive, can help you write your values and views that will guide your life choices. Talking through those values with your Agent offers insights into how you think and make decisions. Your more structured left brain can spell out your specific DO and DO NOT choices about Life-Sustaining Treatments as well as what makes your life worth living. You can list all sorts of decisions you want your Agent to make on your behalf. These can be amended as new developments occur. Just don't die first.

The first four chapters of *Take Care of Dying—Get on with Living* give you four decision clusters which will give you a well-chosen end-of-life experience. You will solve the Puzzle. In Chapter One, you create your Durable Power of Attorney for Health Care in which you name your legal Agent. (Lawyers often call this person your Attorney-in-fact, but it doesn't take an attorney to do the job. "Surrogate" and "Proxy" are also used, but Agent seems simplest for us to use here.) In Chapter Two your Health Care Directive gets specific about your goals and values which support your decisions about treatments you DO and DO NOT want. Chapter Three deals with ways to prepare for unexpected events you don't plan for, and Chapter Four talks about turning terminal—the late phase when different decisions become necessary.

Chapter Five is about communicating your goals, especially with your health care professionals who may use a shared decision-making process with you, leading to better use of Informed Consent. Chapter Six is about managing and updating your records so that after you die your Personal Representative or Trustee can find the documents needed to close your affairs. Chapter Seven looks at ongoing changes as you move through the rest of your life and looks for new ways you can get involved.

Let's get started with taking care of *you* now.

CHAPTER ONE

DURABLE POWER OF ATTORNEY
FOR HEALTH CARE

We talk about the need to respect the wisdom of the old,
yet we treat them like children who could not possibly know
what is best for them. —Susan Jacoby

- **How Do You Choose Your DPOA-HC?**
- **What Do You Want Your Agent To Do For You?**
- **Why Ask Your Agent To Sign a Consent To Serve?**
- **Make Your Choices Official—Document Them.**
- **What Other Resources Do You Want to Have on Hand?**

Six-thirty a.m. the phone is ringing. "Who's calling at this hour, waking me up?" I grump, knowing I'll answer anyway.

"It's your old friend, Sharon," the voice says, "in need of help." Sharon is never in need of help, never wants to have to ask for it. Last time we talked, her mother, who is 90 and lives in New York, had been given three or four weeks to live and was starting to go blind. So I'm all attention.

"Mother has finally agreed to go to the hospital," Sharon says in fast summary.

"But they won't admit her without a signed Agent—someone to act on her behalf—what you've been writing about. So I'm calling you. You know how Mom always refused to talk about any of this. Now it's an emergency and she still hasn't told me or brother Art in Texas what she wants. Just what I figured would happen. So what do I do now?"

This is how we create emergencies by not planning ahead for the inevitable. We can be stubborn, private, scared, silent, resistant, in denial—but the net effect is to leave our family helpless, yet responsible.

Personally, I can relate to her mother. I know I'm strong and can make my own decisions, thank you very much, so I don't really need anyone to do it for me. I've been fiercely independent all my adult life, but even I have to admit that I won't live forever —that I have to choose someone to do things for me when I no longer can. But I want to stay in control. I want someone I can trust to do things my way, to make decisions the same way I would, and to follow through with them as tenaciously as I would. But I don't know many people like me.

HOW DO YOU GO ABOUT CHOOSING THE RIGHT AGENT?

Most people look to family first. Not only is it a normal first reaction, it's a strong cultural norm that has been reinforced by custom, perhaps for centuries. Family takes care of its own. If it doesn't, for whatever reason, the law is likely to involve them anyway.

If you haven't named an Agent, most states have family succession laws which list relatives who, in sequence, are legally bound to take care of end-of-life matters for a family member. Usually, they are in this order:

- Your guardian;
- Your Durable Power of Attorney for Health Care;
- Your spouse;
- Your adult children;
- Your adult brothers and sisters;
- Your parents, a social worker, other.

In many states, where there is more than one living person in a category, such as brothers and sisters, all must agree on the health care decisions. This can be a wake-up call. Many families hold widely varying opinions and are unlikely to agree on anything. This requirement to agree may be what motivates some people to actually name their Agent and Alternate. You can learn about the law in your state by searching Advance Directives. Be sure you get your state's website, not the commercial ones.

CONSEQUENCES OF CHOOSING AN AGENT FROM FAMILY

Consider choosing the person closest to you—your spouse, your committed partner or a trusted family member. There's only one problem with choosing any of these people—you set up a serious, potential, built-in conflict of interest. Consider this scenario.

You, David, are 62 and in the last phases of dying of cancer—what some call "active dying"—which is when you're a week or two from your last gasp. You have named your wife of 40 years, Anna Marie, as your agent—no one else knows you as well nor has taken such good care of you. To her you're way too young to die.

During the last consultation with your long-time specialist, he suggested surgery as a kind of short-term "fix-it." Even though it might prolong your life by as much as six months and should give you significant pain relief, he says there's a possibility you might not survive the procedure. You know your limits. Too many times you've had severe, intolerable pain. Enough. For you, it's time to let go. You're through.

Anna Marie, however, is of a different mind. She can't believe you're "giving up," as she sees it. She needs your strength to keep going. She's afraid of being left alone but won't admit it. She's exhausted but doesn't want to let you go. You've slipped into unconsciousness, unable to refuse the surgery. Anna Marie says YES to your doctor, and he's ready to start your "fix-it" surgery.

So there you are—you're ready to die, Anna Marie wants you alive. As your Agent, she's supposed to say NO to your surgeon, as if she were walking in your shoes. That's a profound conflict of interest to set up for someone you love. Yet people do it all the time without seeming to consider how such a decision can tear a person apart. The vow was "in sickness and in health," but is there no mercy?

Another critical factor is often overlooked. A committed couple often agrees to act as Agent for each other, and they feel snug and smug about that—until one of them dies. Then the survivor, often exhausted and weary, finds him/herself without anyone to serve as his/her Agent. This is where Anna Marie will be after David dies. The process of finding an Agent for yourself at such a time feels like "too much." Who is left to choose from now?

Families are strange herds. Some take care of each other wonderfully well. Others run and hide when the work starts. And they do everything in between. Maybe the family is small, or is a blended family with divorces and remarriages—or has made living-together arrangements where traditional family obligations might be less respected. Family life is different today than it was a generation or two ago.

WHAT IF YOU CHOOSE SOMEONE OUTSIDE OF FAMILY?

You can see pitfalls in choosing someone within your family. The idea of asking someone outside the family may be shocking to many older people, but may not seem so radical to Boomers who tend to be less tradition bound than their parents. In 2010 their age group, born between 1946 and 1964, totaled some 76,000,000 people. Averaged out, they are arriving at age 65 at the rate of 10,000 per day for the next 20 years. We will see a huge demand for Agent services. This is an educational opportunity that may finally break our cultural denial around death and dying that has haunted us for so long.

But that's not the only thing. Another unexpected social change is the increase in the number of people who live alone, as reported by Nathan Heller in 2012.[1] He tells us that today half of U.S. residents are single and a third of all households have just one occupant. This is a huge, long-term change due largely to later marriage, earlier divorce, living longer, and social networking. In 1950, there were some four million single occupant households. By 2012, there were 31 million—almost eight times as many as in 1950. That's a humongous supply of singles who will one day need the services of an Agent. If we start talking about these things now, we just might invent some new modes of community—mutual self-help, caring for each other.

All of which suggests we might consider sources outside the family. Consider choosing a person with health care experience—a nurse or nurse administrator, a social worker, an emergency medical technician. (To be your Agent, this health care professional can't be your doctor or an employee of an institution where you reside. Check your state law.) Their experience, combined with a persistent willingness to listen and learn your future desires, is the kind of support you need in an Agent.

WHAT ARE THE QUALIFICATIONS FOR AN EFFECTIVE AGENT?

In the grid on the next page you can compare three possible Agents on ten qualifications—the first four on availability, five more on decision-making and communication abilities. Use the tenth space for any special requirement you may want. This is an effective way to do a quick but relevant comparison of three people. The person with the most YES responses presumably would be your first choice, the other two people being possible Alternates. Or this analysis may lead you to think of someone else to consider.

Many friends may be glad to serve voluntarily. However, depending on the relationship and whether your state permits it, it's not unreasonable to pay for these services—it's patient advocacy work. This is a new field for which there are schools of varying depth. When I researched patient advocacy training it looked rather thin. No standard curriculum, no degrees, unspecific descriptions of course content, and no licensing at this time. If you decide to go this route you need to be very specific about what skills you are looking for, what results you expect, and you need to have discussions and agreements about these things on a regular, on-going basis. Paying well-informed friends who follow through on commitments may be a better choice—based on qualifications you can identify. Trust may be the key factor.

I have chosen a friend-professional as my Agent. She is licensed as a Certified Professional Guardian and Guardian *ad litem* in Washington State. I didn't know all that when I chose her—my choice was based first on trust. Her work requires her to administer state law on end-of-life health and financial matters for incapacitated cases assigned by the court. In addition, her personal life includes more experience with death—in family and community—than most people have in a lifetime. She also has experience as a hospital chaplain and a spiritual director. She's amply qualified to be a non-family Agent.

When you choose a non-family Agent, let your family know. As we've seen, tradition has long held that family takes care of its own. But we've also seen the conflicts of interest they may produce. It's better to face the issues first by letting them know of your break from tradition and your reasons for making that choice. If they find it hard to accept, this is your first challenge of facing the conflict, just as you will expect your Agent to do under fire. Then pray for acceptance—or the courage to stand your ground under pressure. You're practicing "To thine own self be true," an expression of your belief in your own power as a person. Your decision must be respected. There may be family differences about your care. Everyone should know whom you've chosen to make your health care decisions when you cannot.

QUALIFICATIONS FOR AN AGENT						
Agent's Name	#1		#2		#3	
Compare 3 candidates	Yes	No	Yes	No	Yes	No
1. Meets your state's criteria for serving as a health care proxy.						
2. Is someone you trust with your life, or who has shown that much integrity.						
3. Is younger than you and in good health. Will be around for a while.						
4. Lives close by or can travel to be with you when needed.						
5. Remains calm in stressful situations. Can make difficult choices stick.						
6. Listens to your values, asks "what if" questions to get full, up-dated picture.						
7. Can act on your values, even when different from their own.						
8. Can handle conflicting opinions between health care providers and family members, and still make decisions.						
9. Can be a strong patient advocate if a physician or institution is unresponsive to your needs.						
10. Your special requirement:						
TOTALS						

WHAT ARE YOU ASKING YOUR AGENT TO DO?

Typically, an Agent is given the authority to make all decisions that you would make for yourself, if you were able. That covers a lot of ground. They will be acting "as if in your shoes," so they will get the same medical information you would . They'll confer with your medical team, review your chart, ask questions about treatment options, get second opinions and finally agree to or refuse medical tests or treatments—based on the values you've discussed with your Agent in preparation for this time. The toughest decisions may be about stopping or starting Life-Sustaining Treatments, such as Artificial Nutrition and Hydration, ventilators or feeding tubes. Detailed guides for handling such difficult decisions are outlined in the ABA's *Consumer's Toolkit, Tool 9.* You can download it at *www.abanet.org/aging.* This is powerful stuff—your life is in your Agent's hands. By the way, the American Bar Association has recently issued an excellent, twenty-page resource for new Agents called, *Making Medical Decisions for Someone Else: A How-to Guide.* Find it at *www.abaaging@abanet.org.*

Some powers cannot be delegated to your Agent. These may vary from state to state. In Washington, these include:

- **Any kind of convulsive therapy**
- **Surgery for the sole purpose of psychosurgery**
- **Psychiatric type procedures that restrict freedom of movement**
- **Commitment for mental health treatment, observation or evaluation**
- **Sterilization**

Many states suspend Advance Directives during pregnancy, renewing coverage after birth. However, this is controversial. According to Nancy M. P. King in 1996, "Many states also suspend advance directives during pregnancy, or at least after viability, thus unconstitutionally limiting a pregnant woman's right to refuse treatment."[2]

Whomever you choose and whatever you want done to comply with your state's laws, a sensitive Agent will invite family involvement. But when it becomes difficult, it's important for your Agent to be able to hold her/his ground and negotiate effectively—or simply make the decision and take the heat. Before this time comes, however, your Agent should sign a Consent to Serve agreement—required in some states, not in others.

CONSENT TO SERVE AGREEMENT

What is an Agent's Consent to Serve form and why does it matter? The purpose is to establish the line of responsibility you want to set up. It is evidence to your family and your health care professionals whom you have appointed to speak for you, and that he/she accepts that responsibility. If there's a lawsuit, it is clear whom you want to represent you. As for family, it clarifies any question of who is to be the decision maker, even though family consensus is desired. This document is intended to make an essential link necessary for seeing that your Health Care Directive is followed. It also provides for terminating the agreement.

States call this agreement by various names. North Dakota calls theirs an Acceptance of Appointment. I like Consent to Serve better. Here is a sample agreement using North Dakota's wording, which I have adapted:

CONSENT TO SERVE

I accept this appointment and agree to serve as Agent or Alternate Agent for health care decisions. I understand I have a duty to act consistently with the desires of the Principal as expressed in this appointment. I understand that this document gives me authority over health care decisions for the Principal only if the Principal becomes incapacitated. I understand that I must act in good faith in exercising my authority under this power of attorney. I understand that the Principal may revoke this power of attorney at any time in any manner.

If I choose to withdraw during the time the Principal is competent, I must notify the Principal of my decision. If I choose to withdraw when the Principal is not able to make health care decisions, I must notify the Principal's Alternate Agent and the physician.

_____   _____
Signature of Agent   Date

_____   _____
Signature of Agent   Date

THE DURABLE POWER OF ATTORNEY FOR HEALTH CARE

There are two kinds of power of attorneys. Durable Power of Attorney (DPOA) and plain Power of Attorney (POA). This little box (for nonlawyers) defines Durable/Plain powers that need to be clearly understood.

WHO DECIDES?		
IF	**DPOA**	**POA**
Principal CAN decide	CANNOT decide	CAN decide
Principal CANNOT decide	CAN decide	CANNOT decide

Once you've chosen your Agent, how do you make it official? You have chosen your Agent and Alternate—now you need to officially empower them. In most states, you don't need an attorney to do this—you simply fill out a document. This document may be called the Durable Power of Attorney for Health Care (DPOA-HC), or the Medical Durable Power of Attorney or something similar. It appoints your Agent as your legal voice under the circumstances you describe in the Consent to Serve.

I want to tell you how my personal document evolved. When I moved to Washington State I went directly to an attorney to take care of adjusting my trust and doing my end-of-life documents—not really knowing what I was asking. He asked a few questions, then a week later handed me a package including a 10-page Durable Medical/Health Care Power of Attorney document, and an 11-page Health Care Directive, complete with blue backings. A bit taken aback, I let him explain what was what, not understanding much. We had a signing ceremony with his staff as witnesses, and I went home with official seals and a sizable bill. It led me to ask, "Who has time to read all this stuff in a busy doctor's office?" Answer: no one.

I didn't realize what I had paid for until I selected an Alternate Agent. We met with my Agent so she could explain what the DPOA-HC was all about. We found several provisions that I didn't want and we worked over the whole thing. I asked my Agent to piece together the provisions we wanted to keep. (To be able to do that, she's an unusually well-qualified Agent). As a single person living away from family, I wanted it tight. So it outlines all the essentials.

My Agent and I produced my Durable Power of Attorney for Health Care. I have tweaked it a few times as I gained information. For example, originally I had no provision about surgery. Then one day I read an article about how much excessive surgery was being done on people over 85. So I added the No Surgery provision. As long as I'm able, I can re-decide that—and I did. I later got eyelid surgery.

Witnessing or notarizing this document is not required in Washington State. I chose to do it because it's simple and may be required in some other state where I might travel. I now carry my Advance Directives and POLST with me when I travel.

There is an important connection between the meaning of *Durable* and *Effective Date.* Legally, your Agent won't be able to act for you until you become incapacitated and can't act for yourself. That's where the meaning of *Durable* comes in. Only when you are "out of it" can your Agent act on your behalf. If you regain consciousness and your ability to function, you take back your power to act.

Many laws say that the DPOA-HC becomes effective when you have been examined by both your doctor and a psychologist or psychiatrist, and both of them certify in your medical record that you are unable to make decisions for yourself—that it's time for your Agent to take over. If you have an emergency trauma or are sedated, it may take too long to produce these two consents from busy doctors. You could die waiting.

It's far more practical to just make it ***EFFECTIVE IMMEDIATELY*** upon signing. Then everyone simply uses their own good sense to move ahead making essential decisions under pressure. The level of trust between you and your Agent makes it possible to transfer decision power as the situation demands. It's like a dance, you leading.

If you feel you need some legal safeguards, an elderlaw attorney may be able to help you. What makes elderlaw attorneys different from the garden variety? They are specially trained in matters of vital concern to older people and end-of-life issues. Search to satisfy yourself. Try *www.agingcarefl.org/aging/legal.*

The general rule is that when you die, your DPOA-HC provisions also die. The powers delegated to your Agent end and the work of the Personal Representative or Trustee named in your Will or Trust begins. Usually, people choose someone other than their health care Agents to wind up their health and financial/property matters.

However, some states extend the power of your Agent long enough to handle organ donation, final disposition of your body and other funeral arrangements. This helps if your Personal Representative or Trustee is coming from a distance, or if your death comes sooner than expected and a little time is needed for coordination. Another option is to have a separate Durable Power of Attorney for your Funeral. Family conflict might be an example of a vital need for a separate Funeral DPOA-HC.

There is no standard legal form for your values and decisions. The simplest DPOA-HC document is often your own state's form, which you can find by searching for Advance Directives. Washington's document, only two pages long, details everything you need to comply with the state law—nothing extra—and provides an easy-to-use format.

Many versions of basic DPOA-HC forms, properly signed and notarized, are legal in my state of Washington or your state. Other forms are available online at Caring Connections, End of Life Washington (free or donations requested), or commercial sites like Findlaw, LegacyWriter, LegalZoom, or RocketLawyer. Choose one, follow their instructions, pay the money and they too will be legal in your state.

All this said, the form is not the issue. Your decisions are. Your decisions and the strength of your relationship with your chosen Agent are the key issues. I want to show you the document I developed, in collaboration with my Agent and Alternates. Why am I sharing my personal DPOA-HC with you? For one thing, you may be able to use it to develop your own. For another, my experience may save you both headaches and money.

Many of you may want something simpler. Mine specifics exactly what powers I give my Agent, when they end, and other essential details. We both have a clear understanding of our agreement. That's worth a lot. Here it is on the next pages.

> INSTRUCTIONS TO PHYSICIANS AND HOSPITAL:
> PLEASE PLACE THIS DOCUMENT IN THE <u>FRONT</u> OF MY
> MEDICAL FILE AND KEEP IT JUST BEHIND MY POLST FORM.

<u>DURABLE POWER OF ATTORNEY FOR HEALTH CARE</u>

of

THEODORA F. WELLS

I.

APPOINTMENT OF DURABLE POWER OF ATTORNEY FOR HEALTH CARE

Pursuant to Chapter 11.94 of the Revised Code of Washington, I, THEODORA F. WELLS, as Principal, appoint C.T. (name withheld) as my Durable Power of Attorney for Health Care. If for any reason she becomes unable, unavailable or unwilling to act, I appoint C.B. (name withheld) as my alternate Durable Power of Attorney for Health Care. If C.B. is unable, unavailable or unwilling to act, I appoint N.C. (name withheld) as the alternate.

My Medical Attorneys in Fact, in order of succession, may be found at the following addresses and phone numbers:

	Name	Address	Phone	Cell phone
1	C.T.			
2	C.B.			
3	N.C.			

In the event that none of these are able, available or willing to act as my Durable Power of Attorney for Health Care, I request that the current Director of Enso House, (name, address and phone withheld) be contacted to name another person(s) to act in that capacity for me. That institution shares the values I have listed in my Health Care Directive, and the Director will know who would be a good fit to serve in this capacity for me.

This Durable Power of Attorney for Health Care becomes EFFECTIVE IMMEDIATELY with the signing of this instrument.

II.

AUTHORITY

A. **Authority of Attorney in Fact.** *My agent(s) and I have discussed at length my personal values and medical wishes. These wishes are fully represented in my Health Care Directive* <u>*attached hereto.*</u>

My agent will represent those values and wishes as if I, myself, were making my healthcare decisions at any given time. I direct my healthcare givers to honor her directions as if I, myself, were giving them. I accept the consequences of all directions made by my agent.

This authority becomes EFFECTIVE IMMEDIATELY with the signing of this instrument.

I grant my agent complete authority to make all decisions about my health care. This includes, but is not limited to:

1. Consenting, refusing consent, and withdrawing consent for medical treatment recommended by my physicians, including life-sustaining treatments.

2. Requesting particular medical treatments.

3. Accessing my medical records and information; this release authority applies also to information governed by the Health Insurance Portability and Accounting Act of 1996 as detailed in Part III below.

4. Employing and dismissing healthcare providers.

5. Changing my healthcare insurers.

6. Making or revising a Physician Orders for Life-Sustaining Treatment (POLST) form for me.

7. Removing me from any healthcare facility to another facility, a private home, residential hospice, or other place.

8. Signing any documents, waivers or releases from liability required to implement my wishes, including documents titled or purporting to be a Refusal to Permit Treatment and Leaving Hospital Against Medical Advice.

B.   **Indemnity.** My estate shall hold harmless and indemnify my Attorney in Fact from all liability for acts performed in good faith.

C.   **Competency.** I understand the full import of this directive and I am emotionally and mentally competent to make this directive.

D.   **Prior Directives.** This Directive shall supersede all previous directives including those signed on June 10, 2005.

E.   **Applicable Law.** The applicable provisions of the Revised Code and laws of Washington, as they exist now or as they are hereafter amended, shall govern this Durable Power of Attorney.

F.   **Severability.** It is my wish that every part of this directive be fully implemented. If for any reason any part is held invalid, it is my wish that the remainder of my directive be implemented.

III.

HIPAA DISCLOSURE AUTHORIZATION

A.   **Release Authority.** I intend for my agent to be treated as I would be with respect to my rights regarding the use and disclosure of my individually identifiable health information or other medical records. This release authority applies to any information governed by the Health Insurance Portability and Accountability Act of 1996 ("HIPAA"), 42 U.S.C. §1230d and 45CFR §§160-164, 164-534 of which the Privacy Rules became effective on April 14, 2003.

B.   **Disclosure without Restriction.** I authorize any physician, healthcare professional, dentist, health plan, hospital, clinic, laboratory, pharmacy, or other covered healthcare provider, any insurance company and the Medical Information Bureau Inc., or other healthcare clearinghouse that has provided treatment or services to me to give, to disclose and release to my agent, without restriction, all of my individually identifiable health information and medical records regarding my past, present, or future medical or mental health conditions.

C.   **Prior Agreements.** The authority given my Agent shall supersede any prior agreement that I may have made with my healthcare providers, and shall expire only if I revoke this authority in writing and deliver it to my health-care provider.

D. **Transfer of Authority to Personal Representative.** After my death this HIPAA Disclosure Authorization applies to the Personal Representative(s) appointed in my Last Will and Testament.

IV

DURABLE POWER OF ATTORNEY FOR HEALTH CARE

NOTE: I have purposely not chosen a family member for two key reasons: (1) to avoid any possible conflict of interest; and (2) we all live too far apart, and see each other too seldom, for any of them to be up-to-date and ready to implement my wishes when needed.

A. **Effectiveness.** Because there will be times when I still have capacity, yet want my Attorney to assist me as my medical advocate, this Durable Power of Attorney is EFFECTIVE IMMEDIATELY. IT SHALL REMAIN EFFECTIVE AND IRREVOCABLE DURING ANY PERIOD OF MY DISABILITY OR INCOMPETENCE. I hereby instruct my Durable Power of Attorney to consult with me regardless of the severity of my disability or incompetence, and to encourage me to assist in medical decision-making as fully as I am able. That having been said, during any period of disability or incompetence my Medical Attorney in Fact shall have full authority and responsibility for decisions regarding my healthcare until my competence is restored. After that this instrument shall remain effective until revoked by me.

B. **Duration.** To the fullest extent legally possible, this Power of Attorney shall continue after my death as needed to implement my after-death instructions referred to in my Health Care Directive and other instruments.

C. **How This Power Can Be Revoked or Canceled.** This instrument can be revoked by a written statement to that effect, or by any other expression of intention to revoke. However, if I express disagreement with a particular decision made for me, that disagreement alone is not a revocation of this document.

> **D.**   **Compensation.** My Medical Attorney in Fact shall be entitled to receive compensation for her services rendered at the standard rate applicable for such services in Island County, Washington.
>
> **E.**   **Recording.** It is not necessary to record this document, but if this document has been recorded, then revocation shall be complete only when the revocation is recorded in the Office of the Auditor in the same county.
>
> **F.**   **Copies.** A photocopy or facsimile of the signed original hereof, shall be considered and relied upon as fully as the original.
>
> By signing this document, I indicate that I understand the purpose and effect of this Durable Power of Attorney for Health Care.
>
> Dated this _____ day of _____
>
> _____
> Theodora F. Wells, Principal

You may wish to notarize this document. Each state has its own rules about witnessing and notarizing their documents. Do what your state says.

Yes, all this seems like a lot of work. And it is. But it's like putting together an emergency first aid kit—you don't expect to use it anytime soon, but you're prepared if things get serious. Rounding up your resources will save your Agent, and later your Personal Representative or Trustee, many a headache.

WHAT OTHER RESOURCES WILL YOU WANT ON HAND?

- **First, keep a current list of your medications.** Doctors always ask for it. I keep a list on my computer and update it when my prescriptions change. Keep it in your purse or wallet, or with emergency papers you carry.

- **Second, pull together your professional team—your doctor, attorney and investment counselor.** If you've made a Will or Trust, add the person you have chosen as Personal Representative or Trustee. Now add the names of your Agent and Alternate, and any other specialists you choose for your ongoing team. They should all have copies so they can coordinate with each other as needed.

- **Third, consider setting up emergency access to your money with a Durable Power of Attorney for Finances.** Or if that seems excessive, put your Agent on a checking account in order to access some of your money to pay bills or caregivers when you can't. Have a clear understanding with your Agent about how this account is to be used.

- **Fourth, start making a list of relatives and friends who might be called on to help out in case of emergency.** Include emails and phones. No need to ask their permission now—they can always say NO later. Your Agent will need this, and perhaps certain family members too, should you have an accident or fall.

- **Lastly, investigate long-term health care insurance.** Major changes in our health care system have led to turmoil in this market, causing high premiums. The longer you wait, the more it'll cost you, presuming you want it at all. But then again, some new insurance product may be offered at more reasonable prices.

Congratulations! You've made the first big decision of choosing an Agent. Celebrate a bit before you start working on what you want them to say. Start thinking about the many things you DO and DO NOT want done in the future when you can't function as well as you can today. You'll know more after you complete the next chapter. Then, talk with your family, your Agent, your physician—make noise, get support—do it for a long time. You'll be doing all you can to get your end-of-life wishes honored.

By the way, how did I handle Sharon's pleas for help
at the top of this chapter? I called my Agent—what else?
She knew to check New York law to clear Sharon
as an eligible proxy, with brother Art's consent.
They completed the paperwork online.

CHAPTER TWO

HEALTH CARE DIRECTIVE (LIVING WILL)

Reality is the leading cause of stress among those in touch with it.
—Lily Tomlin

- **If Not Heroic Measures—What?**
- **Life-Sustaining Treatments—What Are They?**
- **Identifying Your Values—Fun and Games**
- **Advance Health Care Directives—What Do We Know?**
- **My Personal Health Care Directive—One Example**
- **What Resources Are Available to Help Do the Job?**

If you haven't thought through—or even faced—what may happen as the end of your life nears, you may think you have it covered with general statements like "No heroic measures" or "Do whatever it takes to keep me alive." Let's see how those ideas play out in real life. Virginia Morris presents a scenario in *Talking About Death*.

> *Scene: New York Presbyterian Hospital, ICU...a semiconscious eighty-five year old woman has a thick ventilator hose blocking her mouth, intravenous lines in her arm and chest, a blood pressure monitor on her finger, and assorted ones running under the sheets to her legs, crotch, and belly. Her eyes are closed. She does not move. A cardiac monitor overhead records the steady rhythm of what remains of her life, beep...beep...beep...*

A nurse outlines her medical history—she is old and weak, with numerous organs in decline—heart, lungs, kidneys. She was brought in initially because of massive internal bleeding and then, having sucked blood into her lungs, she was treated for pneumonia....She is now being treated for...death...all of her systems are failing.

Why is she still receiving all this invasive care? Why don't her family and the doctor let her go? The nurse shrugs. "Her daughter said, 'I don't want to hear about anything bad. I want you to do what you can to fix her.' So we do a little of this and a little of that. We can keep people alive, but we can't necessarily make them better."[1]

If not heroic measures—what? Keeping people alive? Keeping an unconscious person breathing—is that alive? This is what "heroic measures" can look like. This dying woman never specified what treatments she did or didn't want, and apparently she never chose an Agent to act for her when she needed it. Family doesn't seem to want to deal with it. This happens over and over with people who aren't facing their inevitable end and don't make clear, when they have the chance, what they DO or DO NOT want done. Without that, by default, you will probably get whatever it takes to stay alive—and you don't control or decide what that is or what it costs. This leaves you vulnerable to a slow, painful, costly death.

If the doctors have declared you Terminal, that means you have an incurable condition that will likely cause death within about six months. Your "no heroic measures" request shifts responsibility for the next decisions onto your Agent, if you have one, or your family and the health care professionals if you don't. They will substitute their judgments for yours based on what they know about you. You will rely on the doctor to pull something out of his bag of tricks to keep you going, at least for a while. You may dodge making the decision, but you'll get unknown consequences. Doctors have their own values and views; their decisions may not match yours. You lose control when you give away your power this way.

So let's see what's in that doctor's decision-making toolkit. Mostly it's Life-Sustaining Treatments—LSTs.

LIFE-SUSTAINING TREATMENTS, WHAT ARE THEY?

It helps me to look at Life-Sustaining Treatments under two conditions: when you're not Terminal and you'll survive the present problems vs. when you are Terminal, and your physician expects you to die of your underlying disease within six months. When you're not Terminal an LST can help you heal and return to your usual activities. For example, coming out of surgery you may need some kind of airway support to temporarily aid your breathing, but you'll be fine in a few hours or days.

However, when you are Terminal an LST may serve only to prolong your process of dying. While it may relieve pain, its primary purpose is to prolong life functions. If you don't want your life/death stretched out in an Intensive Care Unit or in a Persistent Vegetative State you had better say so while you still can.

It's hard to decide what Life Sustaining Treatments you DO or DO NOT want if you don't know what they are, along with their benefits and risks. Here are brief notes about the most frequently used LSTs.

1. **Antibiotics.** Medicines that help combat infections, but not viruses. Taken orally or intravenously.

   Benefits: Very effective for bacterial infections.

   Risks: If you take more than is prescribed, their effectiveness is reduced. Antibiotics may kill beneficial bacteria needed for normal functioning.

2. **ANH – Artificial Nutrition and Hydration (tube feeding).** ANH is a chemically balanced mix of nutrients and fluids given through a feeding tube that is threaded through your nose or surgically implanted in your stomach. Other people control when and how much you will "eat"—it is not like ordinary food and water taken by mouth.

   Benefits: Provides nutritious feeding when you can't eat or drink normally. Can be maintained indefinitely.

   Risks: If you are dying and your organs are shutting down, your body may not be able to process artificial food and fluids. May cause complications. If you try to remove it, standard protocols may require tying down your hands.

3. Blood transfusions. Intravenous input of processed blood to replace natural blood loss.

Benefits: A safe supply of processed blood is now readily available that can be matched to your blood type, A, B, AB or O, and other factors.

Risks: If it's not properly processed by the supplier, it can carry infections such as HIV. If timely replacement of blood loss does not occur, there will be less blood volume to the brain which increases the risk of a heart attack, stroke or death.

4. Chemotherapy. Taking drug cocktails (for cancer) that kill rapidly dividing cells, especially in bone marrow, digestive tract and hair follicles, leading to fewer blood cells, inflammation and hair loss.

Benefits: Can give you more months of life or, in some cases, eliminate the cancer.

Risks: Can create months of fatigue and poor quality of life without achieving good health.

5. CPR – Cardiopulmonary Resuscitation. CPR is widely taught for helping heart emergencies. CPR is being partially replaced for use by the public by CCC—Continuous Chest Compression, which gives you the best chance of surviving a disruption in blood flow until a defibrillator is available. It is easy to learn and avoids mouth-to-mouth contact.

Benefits: If you're young and healthy, it gives a 40 percent chance of regaining normal health.

Risks: The force required to resuscitate you can break ribs or collapse a lung, especially on elderly persons. If hospitalized for life-limiting diseases like cancer, diabetes or pre-existing heart damage, you have less than a 5 percent chance of surviving and returning to your previous health condition.

6. Dialysis. If kidneys don't work normally, body waste is removed by a machine which filters your blood to rid your body of harmful wastes, extra salt and extra water.

Benefits: Replaces the work of the kidneys and prolongs life.

Risks: You have to do it three times a week, three to fours hours each session. May leave you exhausted.

7. Intubation – or Mechanical Ventilation. This can take several forms: manual support for airway obstruction; a ventilator machine, using a mask for intubation which puts a tube down your throat (very uncomfortable and you can't talk); or a trachcotomy, which is cutting a small hole in your throat, kept open by a tube to give you air, with risks of collapsed lung or bleeding.

Benefits: Oxygen continues to be adequately supplied to your brain. Helps lungs recover from injury or infection. Can be used for permanent breathing support if you can stop talking and you don't mind being dependent on a machine that breathes for you.

Risks: Doesn't help chronic lung problems much. Very uncomfortable. One woman's response to the machine: "Don't ever let them do that to me again. It was like being inhabited by a creature that breathes when IT wants to, not when I want to…. I'd rather die than be breathed for like that."

8. Pacemaker. A small device that is implanted in your chest and heart to regulate abnormal heart rhythms. It uses electrical pulses to prompt the heart to beat at a normal rate, which keeps an adequate supply of oxygen to the brain.

Benefits: By regulating your heart you may have more endurance and energy. Pacemakers can last ten years or more and have become quite reliable.

Risks: A pacemaker can go wrong if the lead gets out of position, if the battery fails, or if the circuits are damaged by exposure to strong magnetic fields.

9. PEG – Percutaneous Endoscopic Gastrostomy. A surgical procedure that implants a feeding tube directly into your stomach.

Benefits: Feeds you when you can't do it yourself. Keeps you alive.

Risks: Usually used in rehab—you're not mobile. It's often presumed that you DO want it unless you say NO in your Health Care Directive. Once started it may be hard to stop.

10. Surgery. Cutting into your body to remove or repair a dysfunction. Intended to help you recover in the best way available. Advance Directives may be temporarily suspended.

Benefits: Medical advances may save lives that couldn't be saved in the past.

Risks: Surgery is a major invasion of the body where a minor error may have major effects on your life. You can't control that, and surgery may be exempted from Advance Directives during the operation. Read the Informed Consent forms you'll be asked to sign. Usually, if there's an error, you (not the physician) end up dealing with the problem.

Now you have an idea of some kinds of medical care you may want to receive or reject when you prepare your Health Care Directive. But how are you going to know what treatments you'll need, and when? We're back to The Puzzle. And we're back to approaching this whole thing by first thinking through your life values, then basing your decisions on those values.

IDENTIFYING YOUR LIFE VALUES

I've always found this effort to be similar to blowing bubbles. They're clear and beautiful; then they disappear. They won't stay put, yet are deep, underlying patterns of life. Here are seven ways I've collected, from general beliefs to here-and-now actions that may help you identify and describe your own values. No data exists as to their effectiveness in identifying a person's values—only you can decide that. So pick and choose what interests you. Take some time with the exercises and you will begin to sort out those values that put ground under your feet as you decide what goes into your Health Care Directive.

1. What Is a Good Way to Describe General Values?

I rummaged around for quite a while with this question but no answer would come. Then one day I remembered my dad, at 81, asking us offspring to give him no more Christmas presents. If we felt like giving, give only things we made ourselves.

I like to write. What could I write for him? I decided to try feeding back to him what he and my mom had taught us—what they believed in enough to invest time, money and energy to teach us. Here is what I came up with.

Oscar B. Westmont

By these lights the man is known
If it's worth doing at all, it's worth doing well
To be productive is to do God's will
Take good care of what you have
Make things last—make things to last
Do your best—no one can ask for more than that
Work is life's therapy—work and time heal all
If they say it can't be done, invent a way
Each family member is a treasure to love and nurture
Count your blessings, not your problems
To make music makes life beautiful
Act on what you believe
Now is the only time there is so live it well
To give of yourself is to truly give
And so it is

I typed this on light brown paper, signed and framed it. He was tickled with it. It was a clear statement of what he and my mother believed in—their values statement.

It faded into the family collection of yesteryears. Twenty-five years later when I went in search of it for this book, I discovered it working its magic, hanging in the garage workshop of a nephew who had made it the opening statement on our family blog.

So this is one way to start defining your values. Ask your kids. They know.

2. How Do You Describe What Makes Your Life Worth Living?

Some people seem to be living to see how long they can live, like wanting to make it to 100. My dad talked that way, but his actions told us more. Each year he spent two or three months working on the family vacation home that he bought for all of us, using his talents to add a loft for extra sleeping space, build an attractive deck, create furniture from driftwood logs or madrona wood and mend fences for safety of grandchildren. The cabin and property were his place to live out his values of pursuing creative ideas and producing quality workmanship in order to give his family a wonderful waterfront vacation spot to time-share. That's what he lived for—family.

Try writing a paragraph or two about your real joys in life. Some topics might be:

Passion: What has been your greatest passion so far? That makes your soul sing?

Profession: What about your work has given you the greatest satisfactions?

Productivity: What makes you want to produce your greatest output?

Pride: What have you done that makes you want to stick out your chest and crow?

Play: What makes you want to dance with joy? To simply have fun? To feel alive?

Go on—get a pencil and a piece of paper and do it!

3. How Do You Describe Your Personal Values?

Most of us have acquired values our parents taught us during our growing up years. These rules may still influence how we make today's decisions. Here are 50 of those teachings that might be influencing you. Try rating them according to their intensity in your life.

Are These My Personal Values?

0=Don't have this rule. 1=Often feel this urge. 2=Yes, that's me!

_____ Be in control of the situation	_____ Be convincing
_____ Be a good team player	_____ Do it by myself
_____ Be right	_____ Appear confident and cool
_____ Be loyal	_____ Be objective, unemotional
_____ Follow your hunches	_____ Be a success
_____ Don't make waves	_____ Be responsible for others
_____ Have the answers	_____ Do the best I'm capable of
_____ Be persistent	_____ Take the initiative
_____ Break rules to see what happens	_____ Follow orders
_____ Keep peace at any price	_____ See that things are done right
_____ Make the boss look good	_____ Be dependable
_____ Be the expert	_____ Be a nice girl/guy
_____ Be logical and rational	_____ Finish it
_____ Stick to my principles, ethics	_____ Go through channels
_____ Be the leader	_____ Make a track record
_____ Be above average	_____ Prove myself
_____ Produce, perform	_____ Be consistent
_____ Be respected	_____ Make myself visible
_____ Be perfect	_____ Be liked, accepted
_____ Improve, develop myself	_____ Be in control of myself
_____ Conform to what's expected	_____ Do not question authority
_____ Be "in the know"	_____ Be first
_____ Be on time	_____ Be prepared for anything
_____ Come out on top, win	_____ Love one another

Do you observe any themes in the rules you scored? Do you have many 1 scores but not many 2s? Or are most of your scores 2s? Is there a theme in your 0 scores? As you review these rules, which ones add to your quality of life? Which ones would you be glad to let go of? You can draw a line through the ones that don't matter much anymore. Or circle the ten you want to take with you when you pass on.

4. How Well Can You Navigate the Activities of Daily Living?

A common means of describing how well you are functioning are two lists used by lawyers and health care professionals. One is about IADL—Instrumental Activities of Daily Living. The other is plain ADL—Activities of Daily Living. It's shorthand for talking about your ability to function in everyday life. Check where your confidence lies.

Instrumental ADLs	Always	Not So Sure	Might Be Slipping
1. Grocery shopping and preparing meals	_____	_____	_____
2. Driving	_____	_____	_____
3. Housework and general cleanliness	_____	_____	_____
4. Managing your money	_____	_____	_____
5. Managing your medications	_____	_____	_____
6. Using the telephone, processing mail and email	_____	_____	_____

Ordinary ADLs			
7. Dressing	_____	_____	_____
8. Bathing	_____	_____	_____
9. Toileting	_____	_____	_____
10. Eating	_____	_____	_____
11. Walking	_____	_____	_____
12. Transferring from bed to chair	_____	_____	_____

Be generous with yourself. Circle the ones you want to work on. Sometimes it gets better! And it points out what is important to you.

5. What Do You Most NOT Want to Die Of?

This ugly question can easily be approached by looking at the top nine causes of death in the U.S. For #10, fill in one more cause of death you really don't want. Then rank order them from worst (10) to least worst (1).

Ranked by Frequency	Ranked by Worst to Least
1. Heart disease	_____
2. Cancer	_____
3. Stroke	_____
4. Chronic Obstructive Pulmonary Disease (COPD)	_____
5. Accidents (unintentional injuries)	_____
6. Diabetes	_____
7. Alzheimer's disease or dementia	_____
8. Influenza and pneumonia	_____
9. Kidney diseases	_____
10. _____ (You choose)	_____

Maybe you don't want to know this information, but at least you can compare some of your fears with those of others and perhaps come out understanding a little more about what health issues are important to you.

6. What Kind of End-of-Life Care Would Please You?

I have a friend who interviews people and puts into words the beliefs or values they hold about how they want their life to end. These quotes may give you some ideas about how you might feel if you are nearing the end of your life. It may help you identify what will be important to you—your values. Circle the dots of those you prefer or add your own special desires.

- Talk to me, not about me. Even if it seems that I cannot hear you, include me in your conversations.

- Help me to remember who I have been. Tell me your favorite memories, stories of our being together, stories of my heritage, stories of my family, stories of how you will remember me. Stories.

- If I am not lucid, but conscious, I would appreciate gentle reminders of my state of mind: tell me I am confused, forgetful, or disoriented. What decisions are you making for me? Please follow my Advance Directives.

- I am pleased that Washington has a Death with Dignity Act. If I am still eligible to end my life in this humane way, please help me do what is legally necessary to make that happen.

- Please play classical music from time to time – Bach, Brahms, Dvorak. Also Debussy and Gershwin. Ensemble chamber music, symphonies or jazz.

- I do not want my caregivers to exhaust themselves in caring for me. Please arrange for respite. If I develop severe dementia, take me to a facility for specialized care. Don't let my disease consume your life.

- I want to make my own decisions for as long as possible. If I now decide differently from my Advance Directives, ask me why I changed my mind. If I seem unconscious, treat me as if I'm present. Please do as I ask.

- I would like medications to control nausea. Also medicate the noisy belabored breathing in my final hours that might be difficult for my loved ones.

- Because I believe in the conservation of resources, keep things simple. Let's appreciate the essence of life as each of us think of it.

- It doesn't matter to me what is done with my body after I die. Do what is simple and expeditious. Whatever is distasteful to my loved ones, don't do.

- I don't want prolonged dying. I want to just go. My idea of a peaceful death is to go to sleep, enter the dream state and not wake up. Please just let me go.

- Don't try to plan my dying. Trust the Lord. Leave it up to Him.

7. When People Can Choose to Die, What Reasons Do They Give?

First, let's make it clear that many believe it's God's business to bring about the ending of their lives. Their values would not let them consider asking for medication to deliberately end their lives. But these values are not shared by everyone. Oregon, Washington, Montana, Vermont, New Mexico and California have now passed Death with Dignity provisions for Terminal persons to go through a careful process to obtain the means to end their lives, which they must self-administer. Oregon and Washington have a history of monitoring this law, which includes reasons given for choosing to die. In what order would you choose for yourself?

Rank Order: 7=Worst, 1=Least Worst

1. Losing autonomy. _____
2. Less able to engage in activities that make life enjoyable. _____
3. Loss of dignity. _____
4. Losing control of bodily functions. _____
5. Burden on family, friends, caregivers. _____
6. Inadequate pain control. _____
7. Financial implications. _____

The important thing is to get clear about your values, to select an Agent who can and will carry forward your values, who can comfortably "walk in your shoes." What, then, is the next step toward that goal? Your values need to be translated into the Advance Directive.

WHAT DO WE KNOW ABOUT ADVANCE DIRECTIVES?

Most states offer little or no help with the essential step of identifying values, but they do provide guidelines for Advance Directives, which brings us to the next question: What health care decisions do most states want you to consider? I can generalize from the information in the 4th edition of *National Survey of State Laws.*[2]

Most state laws have only a few key decisions they want to be sure you make.

Usually, they start and end with forms to fill out, some simple, some more complex. But they all cover only a few basic decisions and not much more. For example, New York's two-page Living Will form provides for five defined major decisions:

NO cardiac resuscitation, NO mechanical respiration, NO tube feeding, NO anti-biotics, and YES to pain relief. On the other hand, some states have more options. Pennsylvania, for instance, has a 16-page set of instructions and forms for both the DPOA for Health Care and Living Will, plus ID cards. They also have a second one based on Catholic values. And Georgia has a full-on workbook with 12 pages of instructions and 14 pages for the Proxy and the Living Will—all in large print. They also suggest using forms from other states. Search your state's requirements online, listed immediately after the paid ads. Follow your state's instructions carefully—it may make a difference about the form's validity.

Many states, like New York, presume you DO NOT want any Life-Sustaining Treatments. Others states presume you DO want Life-Sustaining Treatments and offer their Directive making that assumption. So be very clear about these decisions before you start filling out forms. And read all the details. The main thing to remember is that if you land in a Persistent Vegetative State (PVS), you can be maintained there a long time. It is not a terminal disease. Once you arrive in PVS, you're no longer competent—it's too late to change your mind. So be very careful to make your choices absolutely clear about ANH—Artificial Nutrition and Hydration.

Like Washington, most states have a provision that if you are pregnant, your Directive has no force as long as the pregnancy exists. Also, most states provide that if you are divorced and your spouse was your Agent, that former spouse is automatically discharged from that duty. You'll need to name someone else. Most states give immunity to doctors and Agents when they act in good faith, and they usually honor other states' directives if similar to their own.

When you complete a standard Health Care Directive like your state's form, you are filling out a document that asks the questions the state thinks are important when you're Terminal. But what do *you* think is important? Do you know what Life-Sustaining Treatments they are talking about? Do you know what it's like to be in a Persistent Vegetative State, or your odds of getting out of it? Are these decisions more important to you than, say, giving permission to kill your pain, even if it speeds up your death?

Living Wills developed by states are usually limited to a few Terminal decisions. But many people die without ever having been declared Terminal. We don't all die of chronic diseases. For example, traumatic accidents occur at all ages. And take me: I'm 90, have been sedentary most of my life with a history of a heart attack, two cardioversions, high blood pressure and congestive heart failure. But I have not been declared Terminal. My doctors don't expect me to die within 6 months from heart-related conditions—or anything else. But I'm a natural for it anyway. So I want to provide for myself before my doctor sets up the warning signal of Terminal. You can specify your desires that cover all such situations, at any age. My Health Care Directive includes many pre-terminal decisions. I can't predict what will happen to my health or when it will happen, so I put all the end-of-life decisions I can think of in one place. My Agent can sort out the rest when the time comes.

What personal goals do you want to express? Perhaps your parents were victims of Alzheimer's disease and you are worried it might pass on to you. What degree of control can you keep when you fear losing your mind? Or, take my scenario of having a heart attack. What about CPR? When is resuscitation (and what kind of resuscitation) safe for me? Cancer patients have many decisions to make. I know several people with cancer who have decided not to continue chemotherapy. They no longer feel that their quality of life would be improved if it were sustained that way. They fear chemo might be harder on their bodies than on the cancer itself. Each case is different, each treatment is different, and each of us must decide for ourselves, in consultation with our doctors, which treatments or withdrawal of treatments best suits our values and goals at the time. They're always subject to change. I suggest you state what you want, even though you may not get it. But you're on record. That improves your odds. Perhaps one day our decisions will have legal standing.

Now we are ready for action: How do you use all this information in writing your own Health Care Directive? I can answer that best by sharing an example—my own Health Care Directive along with some of the reasoning that gave it shape.

The directives marked with emojis are cross-referenced in the Health Care Directive on pages 42 through 44.

⊘ If I am being treated at a facility that adheres to…Ethical and Religious Directives for Catholic Health Care Services…(ERDs), or any other religious customs or beliefs…. Some of the finest health care is delivered in Catholic and other religious health care facilities. Many places it's the only care available. This would not bother me if I were of that faith, but what if I am not? My principle concern is that my Advance Directive be honored. One Catholic directive states that "the free and informed health care decision of the person…is to be followed so long as it does not contradict Catholic principles."[3] Another repeats this condition: "… the free and informed judgment made by a competent adult patient concerning the use or withdrawal of life-sustaining procedures should always be respected and normally complied with, unless it is contrary to Catholic moral teachings."[4] Yet, when I asked at a Catholic hospital if these directives would mean a Catholic health care facility would NOT honor a patient's Advance Directive, the response was, "No, it does not." I was told there may be an occasional situation, such as some patients in a Persistent Vegetative State, when the patient has requested something in his/her Advance Directive that is not consistent with the moral teachings of the Church. In these few cases, a Catholic health facility would not be able to comply.

Well, which is it? Yes or No? As a non-Catholic, spiritual person who is concerned with avoiding PVS, I choose to make my own decisions on these matters.

Search Catholic Ethical and Religious Directives for answers to your own questions.

🚫 I DO NOT want restraints of any kind…. In my research, restraints have been mentioned mostly when someone resists tube feeding or is out of control. If it's about a stomach tube, I'd be trying to say "Get rid of it." If otherwise, ask my Agent what to do—she can translate because she knows my values. That's why she's there.

☺ I DO authorize any procedures that may speed up the natural process of dying…. When my time has come, I have no interest in lingering. My concerns will be about pain reduction and comfort care—and probably finances.

☺ I DO want to use the Death with Dignity Act, if I am eligible. I am thankful that my State of Washington saw fit to pass our Death with Dignity Act giving me, under certain conditions, more options about how I die. I hope I'm eligible—you have to be terminal, competent, not depressed, and able to self-administer the potion. I deeply believe this option should be available to all who believe it's a viable choice. Likewise, since it goes against Catholic moral teaching, rejection of this option should be (and is) available to them. One of my values is to honor each others' beliefs and choices, even when we don't agree. I would hope for reciprocal respect.

☺ I DO want my body to be cremated....To me, the coffin is a thing of the past and takes up too much ground. When we were burying my father the cemetery called to find out if we wanted insurance. I asked, "What for?" Reply: "Well—to guarantee the seal on the casket." I shot back: "Who's going to dig it up to find out?" That ended that. Burial or cremation is a deeply personal choice, influenced by one's values, customs and religious beliefs. Today we have another choice—green burials.

I think it's a courtesy to make advance funeral arrangements, but not prepay them. In my opinion, it's not a good investment. You may move as I did, or the funeral home may not be in business by the time you die. Better to set up a Paid-On-Death bank account, or something similar. I prefer to keep the mortuary out of my purse.

☺ I DO want my ashes scattered, not buried.... Again, a highly personal choice. Our vacation property is a great place to scatter my ashes to the winds and free my soul. Just think: we can choose our own way of leaving this world. What an incredible touch of grace our freedoms give us.

And finally, what are the values on which this Directive is based? The first page gives my general philosophy, with bold emphasis on my brief values statement:

To me, to be alive is to be able to read, write, speak out, learn, share and care among others in community. If I cannot do so, it is time to move on to a more fruitful continuance of soul growth. To me, that transition is death.

This values statement explains what I need to feel alive. When my body won't perform the functions it takes to support these values, life won't be worth living.

Having been addicted to a sedentary life, things athletic and outdoors are not in my experience so they don't appear here. Other things that I love, such as playing the piano, are vital to me, but I could let go of that if I can have my reading and writing. This statement may change as I get nearer to the end of my life, but I'm already 90 and this statement is still working. It might change when I'm less able to get around, or if my mind goes. We'll see....

Here is my personal Health Care Directive (emojis are included to cross reference comments on pages 42 to 44).

HEALTH CARE DIRECTIVE

of

THEODORA F. WELLS

(Pursuant to RCW 70.122)

(To be attached to Durable Power of Attorney for Health Care)

To my family, to my friends, to my healthcare personnel and facilities, and especially to those whom I have chosen to represent me in medical decisions when I no longer have full capacity to represent myself:

Because I cannot know what circumstances will befall me and this body of mine, and because I cannot know what technical or ethical decisions may need to be made on my behalf, it is pointless to decide now on the medical minutiae I might or might not need in the future. Therefore, this Health Care Directive serves as the basis for end-of-life decisions to be made by my Durable Power of Attorney for Health Care.

I completely trust my Durable Power of Attorney for Health Care, (name and phone number withheld) to make those moment-to-moment decisions in consultation with my medical providers and immediate family. I want to avoid guardianship. To avoid any conflicts of interest, especially among family, final decisions rest with my Durable Power of Attorney for Health Care, or Agent, whose fairness I trust.

Death is as much a reality as birth, growth, maturity and old age; however, it should not include the indignity of useless deterioration, dependence and hopeless pain. It should include the dignity of each person, as much as possible, making their own end-of-life decisions, including use of the Death with Dignity Act.

To me, to be alive is to be able to read, write, speak out, learn, share and care among others in community. If I cannot do so, it is time to move on to

a more fruitful continuance of soul growth. To me, death is that transition. I understand that a physician probably cannot translate this statement into medical decisions when I am unable to make decisions for myself. That is why I have chosen (name withheld) as my Agent. She can make that translation for me. She knows well enough how I would decide any medical or health questions.

The book I am writing, *Take Care of Dying—Get On With Living,* speaks boldly about how to take as much control as possible over one's own end-of-life decisions. The decisions listed below are based on extensive research, study and discussion and I expect them to be followed, as provided in the Washington State Natural Death Act (RCW 70.122.) I have discussed these values and decisions at length with my Agent and Alternate(s), and fully trust their judgment when acting in my stead.

Please consult my POLST (Physician Orders for Life-Sustaining Treatment) form for the clearest understanding of my choices for emergencies. Further decisions include:

I DO NOT want cardiopulmonary resuscitation (CPR) or defibrillation.

I DO NOT want intubation. Manual airway support is acceptable for short times.

If my heart stops and/or my breathing stops, DO NOT BRING ME BACK FROM DEATH only to make me have to go through it again at a later time.

I DO NOT want any treatment that would risk putting me into a persistent vegetative state (PVS) or other similar condition.

I DO NOT want my dying process prolonged for any reason.

I DO NOT want to be put on a ventilator or a respirator, even for a short term.

I DO NOT want any artificially provided long-term (two weeks or more) nutrition or hydration. I DO NOT want feeding tubes at any time.

⊘ If I am being treated at a health care facility that adheres to the Ethical and Religious Directives for Catholic Health Care Services (ERDs), or any other religious formulation, admission to such an institution does NOT constitute my implied consent to any of their rules that are in conflict with my Advance Directive. If they decline to follow any of my wishes as set out in this Health Care Directive, I DO direct that I be transferred in a timely manner to a hospital, nursing home, hospice or other institution, which will agree to honor my instructions. My first choice would be (name of hospital and city).

🚫 I DO NOT want restraints of any kind placed on my body, arms, legs or head. If I am resisting treatment that much, I am refusing the treatment(s) being offered.

☺ I DO authorize any procedures that may speed up the natural process of dying, which by definition I consider to be "physician-assisted dying," distinct from what some may label "physician-assisted suicide" or "mercy killing" or "euthanasia." I instruct that my caregivers be held harmless from any liability resulting therefrom.

☺ I DO want to use the Death with Dignity Act, if I am eligible.

I DO want antibiotics to counter bacterial infection.

I DO want vigorous treatment to relieve pain and to make me comfortable, even if this might unintentionally hasten my death or make me unconscious or cause me to become addicted. Should any question arise in this regard, I instruct that my caregivers be held harmless from any liability resulting therefrom.

I DO NOT want surgery. I am too old and have too many interacting conditions to make the risks worthwhile. If pain is the problem, give me more morphine and let me go in comfort and peace. I DO NOT want "heroic efforts" to prolong my life. My Agent can make exceptions as seem appropriate in her opinion.

If I should suffer irreversible heart or brain damage, or something comparable,

I DO NOT want surgery or ICU-level of care. At that point, or earlier, I DO want hospice and peaceful end-of-life care.

I DO NOT want to die in a nursing home. I DO want to die at my home or in a homelike environment, preferably at Enso House, (phone number).

I DO NOT want to leave any anatomical gifts.

I DO NOT want an autopsy.

☺ I DO want my body to be cremated, which I have arranged through the (Name of agency), membership number, call-on-death (phone number).

☺ I DO want my ashes scattered, not buried, as described in my personal essay.

WHAT RESOURCES ARE AVAILABLE TO HELP DO THE JOB?

To complete your Health Care Directive package there are several add-on documents available if needed. All are one-page documents except for #6.

1. Hospital Visitation Authorization—for singles or gay/lesbian partners.

2. Provision for when a health care provider refuses to honor any part of your Health Care Directive. It says you are to be removed to a facility that will honor them.

3. Dementia Provision.

4. My Particular Wishes.

5. Designate an Agent for Funeral Arrangements.

6. Alzheimer's Disease and Dementia Mental Health Directive, 2013. Described at *endoflifewa.org*. Available by snail mail. Cost of producing and mailing is $10. Donation appreciated.

The last step—put it in writing. You may want to get your end-of-life planning done in as short a time as possible. If so, I suggest you use your state's forms—they provide the fewest choices, many focusing on the key issue of YES or NO for artificial nutrition and hydration. Here are some options, listed by the least to the most number of decisions.

Note: None of these documents include Emergency Medical Services.

1. **Advance Directive forms in your state's laws**. Perhaps the easiest to access and complete, but may leave out many items you want to include. Search Natural Death Act or Living Wills in your state. Cost: Free.

2. **Caring Connections has forms for each state.** Updated by National Hospice and Palliative Care Organization (NHPCO) funded by Robert Wood Johnson Foundation following a major study of how we die in America in late 1990's. Search Caring Connections. Cost: Free.

3. **Online legal services** like Findlaw, LegacyWriter, LegalZoom, RocketLawyer. Usually, you can't see what provisions these resources offer before completing and committing to pay. They may not give you all the options you want. By the way, Nolo Press is a useful reference. Search by vendor. Cost estimate: Varies.

4. **Five Wishes** – a very popular booklet. Specify clearly what you DO and DO NOT want, even if you should get into a PVS. If you don't state your limits, you are likely to get all Life-Sustaining Treatments that apply. It offers preferences for personal end-of-life comfort care. Easy to use. Available in 26 languages. Not valid in eight states: AL, IN, KA, NH, OH, OR, TX, and UT. *www.agingwithdignity.org*. Cost: $5.00 each.

5. **End of Life Washington Combined Form** – The best of all, in my opinion, except for what I put together for myself (I have a bias). Their values are much like mine, they have covered all the bases, have excellent instructions, and they update it promptly when needed. If I had known about it when I started my searches, I might not have gone further. It takes the least time to gain the most results. Download it at *endoflifewa.org*. Cost: Donation requested.

6. **My Health Care Directive in this chapter.** It takes more time to compose your own values. Choose whatever ideas you want from my Directive, substituting your own decisions based on your values. Cost: Free.

If you're rushed, try one of the simpler forms, then come back and do a more personalized directive after you've thought about it more. But get something down in writing—selection of your Agent and limits on your worst fears. Talk with your Agent. Then do a more complete document a little later and continue talking with your Agent.

You now have the information you need for most of your Advance Care Planning, except for what to do in emergencies—any accident or unexpected disability. That's in "Chapter Three: Unexpected Events You Didn't Plan For."

CHAPTER THREE

UNEXPECTED EVENTS YOU DIDN'T PLAN FOR

If you're prepared, you won't need it. If you're not, you will. — *Theo Wells*

- **POLST: What Is a "Physician Orders for Life-Sustaining Treatment"?**
- **Where Does Medicare Stand on End-of-Life Talks?**
- **Can Advance Directives Be Suspended by Surgery Centers?**
- **Iatrogenic Diseases: Surviving the Medical/Hospital Systems**
- **Death by Disease Is Our Last Unexpected Event**

After decades of struggle to improve end-of-life care and to give patients' wishes some power over the long reach of medical technology, an increasing number of U.S. health care professionals are supporting a new way to slice through the confusion, pain and sadness that can surround a hospital or nursing home death.

The emerging solution is a medical order form that instructs health providers to honor a patient's wishes—ranging from simple comfort care to the most intense and heroic measures. The document, originating in Oregon in 1991, is known as a POLST— Physician Orders for Life-Sustaining Treatment.[1]

Health care professionals gathered to develop the first POLST form that would give patients more control over their end-of-life decisions. It took a while for training, ongoing education and quality improvements on the proposed POLST form for it to be implemented in various health care organizations. Initially Oregon Health and Science University distributed the new form in Oregon and conducted widespread training. Eventually all hospices and a majority of nursing homes were using it successfully. Other states took note.

New York, Pennsylvania, Washington, West Virginia and Wisconsin jumped in early and developed similar programs. As of February 9, 2016, there were 19 endorsed states, approved by the National POLST Paradigm Task Force, the organization that helps states meet the criteria for their new systems. These states are California, Colorado, Georgia, Hawaii, Idaho, Iowa, Louisiana, Maine, Montana, New York, North Carolina, Oregon, Pennsylvania, Tennessee, Utah, Virginia, Washington, West Virginia and Wisconsin. Another 25 states were in the process of developing their programs. Only 1 state, South Dakota, had no program in progress; all other states plus the District of Columbia were in some stage of program development and had contact information listed with the National POLST Paradigm. A concerted effort is under way to assist more states to work through whatever hurdles remain to get aboard. The POLST is usually accepted by all health care facilities in each state, particularly those where the POLST has been in place for some time.

So why is the POLST needed? I have a friend who answered that question in the story she told me not long ago. I've heard many such stories; I'd like to share this one.

The first time I dialed 9-1-1, I only knew that Dean wasn't getting air and we needed help fast. I didn't know this was called an air hunger attack, and I didn't know how close he would come to dying.

When the medics showed up I relaxed. They would take him to the Emergency Room where he would get some magical meds and everything would be all right. "I'll be along shortly," I told Dean as they wheeled him away. It looked like a long day ahead, so I took my time getting ready to leave the house—I chose a comfortable but stylish outfit, dabbed on a bit of makeup, put a few curls in my hair and packed some clothes for Dean's trip home. All the while, I knew Dean would be fine.

When I got to the hospital, the ER nurse—a friend of mine—told me the truth: Dean's heart had stopped twice before he even got to the hospital. And the tubing I saw spread out on the table beside his bed had been scheduled to be inserted down his throat and attached to a machine—a ventilator, she called it—that would pump air into his lungs. But seconds before I walked in, his airways had opened and he was breathing again. After three days in Critical Care he put on his clothes and we drove home.

Close call, but it opened the window to what we could expect in the future. I found out about ventilators. "They do a lot of good in some cases," my friend the nurse had said. "The problem would be getting him off it." With lungs as severely compromised as Dean's, I learned the chances of his ever breathing on his own would be next to nil, once he was intubated—the term they use for connecting someone to a ventilator. I learned, too, that intubation can be torture for a human who is conscious or even semi-conscious. Talking and swallowing are out, discomfort is unbearable, but the patient must bear it because he has no choice.

We talked it over, Dean and I, and the decision was unanimous: NO INTUBATION. No way was my husband going to spend his last hours—or days—in that macabre condition.

Six months later, before dawn, our bedroom was full of EMTs again. "NO INTUBATION!" I told them as they prepared Dean for the gurney.

"Do you have a POLST form, Ma'am?" asked the lead EMT.

"No." I could find out what he was talking about later. For now I had to get dressed—yesterday's jeans, baggy sweatshirt, no bra. If this was the end, I needed to be with Dean. And I had to make sure no one put a tube down his throat.

The attack was fierce and Dean fought hard. The respiratory therapist gave him everything in the arsenal. When the arterial blood test showed his CO_2 level at 84—well over twice what it should have been—the ER doctor told the nurse to prepare for intubation.

"NO INTUBATION!' I said, but the doctor insisted. We stepped into the hall.

"We are going to keep trying the meds," I said. "And if it doesn't work, you are going to give him enough morphine to calm him. But you are NOT going to put that tube down his throat."

The doctor went to my husband's side and asked if he would like to have a machine breathe for him. "You won't have to struggle like this any more," he said. "You will be able to relax and get some good rest." Dean's head bobbed up and down in agreement; he would have agreed to having a rattlesnake threaded down his throat if it promised him relief from his battle for breath. Surely the doctor could see my husband was in no condition to make a rational decision.

The doctor turned to me in triumph. "There, you see?" he said. "I will take my orders from the patient."

In desperation I looked at the respiratory therapist standing by. "If this were your father...?"

"I'd give the meds a little longer," he answered.

I stood my ground, the meds worked, and Dean started pulling oxygen into his lungs. But we had come so close to the intubation Dean had so dreaded.

That day I learned all about the POLST.

WHY THE POLST IS SO USEFUL

Here's why the POLST is so useful. It is:

- **Actionable.** A signed medical order is actionable immediately after it's signed.

- **Portable.** It travels with you everywhere, from home to other health care facilities, from home to another home, to another state where it may be honored.

- **Visible.** Its bright color, usually electric pink, is easy to identify.

- **Flexible.** Changes can be made *en route,* if it becomes necessary.

- **Acceptable at most health care facilities,** even if signed by a doctor not on staff.

- **Voluntary in all states endorsed by the National POLST Paradigm Program,** and usually must be signed by you as well as your medical professional.

"It gives you power and portability," says Sally Denton, an RN who helped develop the POLST. "For a patient, the new form is like a suit of armor, making sure that all medical workers, in all settings, respect your wishes."[2]

On the POLST you can choose if you want CPR, what level of hospital care you wish, whether to use artificial nutrition and hydration, whether to be intubated, whether to use dialysis, and some states include use of antibiotics. Let's concentrate for a moment on CPR which has been the most common Life-Sustaining Treatment offered under most existing emergency systems.

CPR—cardiopulmonary resuscitation—is the paramedic's primary rescue tool. When 9-1-1 is called it often means someone can't breathe or is having a heart attack. The ambulance arrives and paramedics are expecting to resuscitate someone unless there's a signed order not to do so. Asking emergency personnel not to attempt resuscitation may be a difficult decision for you and your doctor to make. But it may be even harder for paramedics who are intensely trained to save lives this way.

Dr. Robert Shmerling of Beth Israel Deaconess Medical Center suggests that CPR's success rate has been vastly overstated, largely due to early TV shows like "Emergency!"[3] Most victims in TV dramas are young and require CPR following a trauma or near drowning—conditions with the highest success rates. The first few minutes are critical. Here's what can happen if you are generally healthy, not a frail elderly person, according to Dr. M.S. Eisenberg in *Resuscitate! How Your Community Can Improve Survival from Sudden Cardiac Arrest.* During the first 4 minutes, your chances of survival are about 40 percent. Defibrillator shocks may be all you need. During those 4 minutes, you probably are going to use the oxygen already in your blood. Once that's used up, you shift to the second phase, where CPR is vital for restoring oxygen to your brain. Every minute, your survival rate drops about 5 percent as you lose more oxygen going to your brain. This phase lasts about 6 minutes, after which you enter the phase where no known therapies are effective. In other words, you're dead, or close to it.[4] However, Amy Vandenbroucke, executive director of the National POLST Paradigm (see POLST online), noted one exception in a private communication with me in 2013: if you are a frail elderly person in a long term care facility, the odds of surviving CPR is less than 3 percent from the beginning.[5]

Studies cited in the Compassion and Support at the End of Life website shows these CPR success rates: up to 30% effectiveness when given outside the hospital; 15% for hospitalized patients; less than 5% for elderly victims with multiple medical problems; and less than 1% for patients with advanced chronic illness.[6] Most CPR is still performed on sick, older people with cardiac disease. In real life, many of those who are revived by CPR wind up being severely debilitated.

By the way, when they talk about that less than 5 percent survival rate, they mean survival between the bed and the hospital door. Nothing is said about surviving long enough to have a meaningful life on the other side of that door. Having the option of "Do Not Attempt Resuscitation" during an emergency can become very important, especially to old folks like me who don't want to risk becoming severely debilitated, or "a vegetable," as in a Persistent Vegetative State (PVS).

Some survive in a PVS, which may make them eligible for the "Zone of Indistinction." This means you are on one or more Life-Sustaining Treatments: a breathing machine, a tube feeding directly through your stomach wall, an IV dripping into your hand, or other life-sustaining procedures. Then they move you to a quiet ward of the hospital or a rehab facility—a Zone of Indistinction—to service your remaining functions in peace. You can stay there a long time. PVS is not a terminal condition. And it's expensive. S.R. Kaufman tells about it in *And a Time to Die: How American Hospitals Shape the End of Life.*[7] Terri Schiavo was in the Zone for 15 years.

Back to the POLST. Most states designate places in your home where paramedics can expect to find your POLST. I have copies of my POLST by my bed, on the refrigerator, near the front door. In addition, in case I'm in trouble away from home, I have copies in my purse, in the glove compartment of my car, on file at the local hospital, with my primary care physician, and with my various specialists. I went overboard, but I figured my POLST would be followed only if it's easy to find.

States can choose alternate names for the POLST that best suit their constituencies. Each state may have different internal concerns or opinions about the POLST.

New York's is MOLST, Medical Orders for Life-Sustaining Treatment. But North Carolina wanted only MOST, Medical Orders for Scope of Treatment. POST is the choice for Idaho, Tennessee and West Virginia, Physician Orders for Scope of Treatment. Several states seem to want to eliminate the Life-Sustaining Treatment concept in the title. Most states choose a hot pink color, only Washington has chosen lime-green, and Wisconsin yellow. Basically, they're all the same form, modified to fit local needs and preferences.

Whichever system your state uses, if you checked Do Not Resuscitate, you will still get comfort care. Do Not Resuscitate does not mean Do Not Treat. DNR means the same as AND: Allow Natural Death. If you're dying, comfort care may include suctioning your airway, administering oxygen, splinting, controlling bleeding, providing pain medications and even giving emotional support.

We can see POLST is a device whose time has come. During our "inventive period" of 1975-2005 many Life-Sustaining Treatments (LSTs) were being developed. (See Appendix: Historic Changes 1975 to 2005.) At first they were seen as a blessing, life extension being the goal of the day. It reflected our national obsession with eternal youth and immortality. As a nation we did not want to think we might die some day. Death was undiscussable. Doctors were just as silent on the topic as their patients. They focused on saving lives because, to them, death symbolized failure. CPR and other LSTs would often extend life. But patients weren't used to saying NO when offered care they didn't want. Or perhaps they didn't want to refuse something they might want later.

About this time states were developing Durable Power of Attorney for Health Care and Health Care Directives (living wills). Then came the Patient Self-Determination Act of 1990, which required hospitals and nursing homes to offer their new patients information about these documents. This major breakthrough gave people the power to decide how they wanted their lives to end. Hospitals gave this information to sick people as they entered the hospital, many of whom were already fearful they might die. Perhaps it was a little late to be thinking of Health Care Directives. So the concept didn't catch on with patients at first. But it soon became apparent that too many people were dying in ways they didn't want.

Doctors most often suggest the POLST for those patients with serious illness or frailty "for whom a health care professional would not be surprised if they died within one year."

If you haven't done so already, this is the time to have that first end-of-life talk with your health care professional—and when you two might write your first POLST.

SO WHERE DOES MEDICARE STAND ON THAT TALK
WITH YOUR DOCTOR?

As you probably know, a few years ago these end-of-life talks were dubbed "death panels" and were removed from Medicare coverage. But let's take a jaunt backward in time to 2009, to La Crosse, Wisconsin, a town of some 52,000, where nearly everyone of a certain age had an Advance Directive. This rare condition came about through consistent efforts of the town's largest hospital, Gundersen Lutheran Health System, a pioneer in insuring that care provided to their patients in their waning days complied with those patients' wishes. Alec MacGillis recorded the conversation in the Washington Post at the time.

Under the leadership of Bernard "Bud" Hammes, Ph.D., a medical ethicist, the hospital took the lead in seeking to have Medicare compensate physicians for consulting with patients on end-of-life planning. They began urging families to plan while they were still healthy. Hammes helped people define the conditions under which they would no longer want life-saving treatments. He found that people would often define this as "when I've reached a point where I don't know who I am or who I'm with, and don't have any hope of recovery." The hospital made it clear that doctors were expected to follow Advance Directives. Along with the other large hospital in town, Franciscan Skemp, more than 90 percent of the people in town had directives when they died. The prevailing attitude among these stoic folks was something like, "We all die and we want to do so with the most dignity and most control. It seems a no-brainer. And it spares our children from making those decisions." Hammes said the family can let go, knowing "that what they do is not only legally right, but personally right." The conversations did not promote any treatment options. According to Hammes, "We're not trying to talk them into anything. We're trying to understand their values and goals, and tell them what medical science can and can't do." He added, "In our community, people don't want to die hooked up to machines."

For this to happen, "there needs to be more than one conversation. But these take a lot of time, a good hour perhaps, plus follow-up talks to make changes as medical situations evolve. Medicare does not reimburse doctors for the time spent on such discussions."[8]

Backed by their success in 2009, Gundersen Lutheran and a few other hospitals set out to change the federal rules. About then Rep. Earl Blumenauer (D-Ore.) submitted legislation that included a provision to reimburse doctors for end-of-life consultations. Shortly after, Democrats added similar language in their health reform bill.

Soon the uproar began. Sarah Palin launched her "death panels" rhetoric; Sen. Charles E. Grassley (R-Iowa) worried about "pulling the plug on Grandma"; and former Speaker of the House, Rep. Newt Gingrich (R-Ga.) was critical—after he had formerly expressed appreciation for the end-of-life care his father-in-law had received at Gundersen. Rep. Paul D. Ryan, (R-Wis.) suggested it was all right for Gundersen to innovate in these directions, but not for the federal government to endorse end-of-life planning.

Not wanting to risk the entire legislation, word came in December, 2010, that the White House was willing to drop the provision, as reported by Robert Pear in the *New York Times*.[9] And so it was until Rep. Earl Blumenauer (D-Ore.) reintroduced it in Congress in March of 2013, opening a new round of "Death Panel" controversy, as reported by Kate Pickert in *Time U.S.*[10] (By the way, Politifact rated the "death panel" meme as its Lie of the Year in 2009.)

Gradually, death panels turned into Death Cafés, designed to breathe life into conversations about dying. "Who would want to?" you might ask. Well, people all around the world are doing it. NPR's Deena Prichep covered it in a 2013 broadcast. It got started by Jon Underwood, a British web designer and self-named "death entrepreneur" who was trying to thread the taboo topic into the conversation. "In continental Europe, there's a tradition of meeting in public places to talk about important and interesting subjects," he says. "So there's a café *philo,* which is a philosophical café, and a *café scientifique.* Bernard Crettaz, a Swiss sociologist, set up a *café mortel,* or death café."[11]

In 2010, Underwood held his own café in the basement of his home, serving tea and cake. His mother, a psychotherapist, facilitated the conversation. "When people sit down to talk about death, the pretense kind of falls away, and people talk very openly and authentically. For English people to do that, with our traditional stiff upper lip, is very rare."[12]

Underwood set up some loose guidelines for death cafés and launched a website. Soon more than 60 death cafés had been held across the world, from Columbus, Ohio, to Eastern Australia.

"When we acknowledge that we're going to die, it falls back on ourselves to ask the question, 'Well, in this limited time that I've got, what's important for me to do?'" says Underwood.[13] It ends up being about not so much how we die as how we live.

A more intimate version of the café idea is to have a conversation about death over dinner. In 2013 Rebekah Denn quotes the co-founder of Let's Have Dinner and Talk About Death, Michael Hebb of Seattle. "How we end our lives is the most important and costly conversation America isn't having….We talk about war and the environment but we don't talk about death. Of all these issues that face us, death is the most certain."[14] He was inspired to start his organization after he heard a pair of doctors on a train ride comment that Americans weren't dying the way they wanted, that "end-of-life expense" was the number one reason for bankruptcy in the U.S., and that over 75 percent of people want to die at home but only 25 percent do.

It doesn't have to be a café or dinner. I recently went to a local end-of-life discussion billed as "What You Always Wanted to Know…but Were Afraid to Ask." This first-time announcement drew about 40 people, hosted by a local hospice doctor. For two hours we explored all concerns that anyone brought up. You could feel the fear evaporate and the confidence grow. All they needed was space for talk, mutual respect and privacy.

And that is exactly what aging people need—end-of-life talks with their doctors. But the doctors need to be paid for their service. Good news came August 31, 2014, on Page 1 of the *New York Times* in a major story called "Coverage for End-of-Life Talks Gaining Ground." And it looks promising when the American Medical Association creates billing codes for this service. It is a legal illusion to think that having a single conversation and filling out a form is enough.

As you get better informed, you may choose not to use all the Life-Sustaining Treatments available to you. Some people might start refusing lifesaving care altogether. Repeated trips to the ICU, pain, pain, pain, plus other exhausting experiences can wear you down. But that is a choice that is yours to make, even though others may want you to hold on until the bitter end. I saw one friend ease into his death when the person dearest to him stopped fighting it and gave him permission to leave. He sighed, relaxed, and slipped away peacefully.

Some unexpected events come in strange shapes and forms. One happened to me. As a patient, I was at the mercy of the system we're in. Here's a personal story.

About a year ago, I had sat through a two-hour meeting. When I stood up to leave, my blood seemed to stay sitting down. I felt faint, started to swoon, and was grateful we had two nurses in the group. They sat me down, called 9-1-1, and saw me off in an ambulance. The hospital emergency department found I needed three pints of blood, cause of blood loss to be determined. After the transfusion, a hospital emergency doctor did an endoscopy. They ran a tiny camera on the end of a flex-tube down my upper digestive tract and found gastrointestinal bleeding, blood coming through many tiny pinpricks in my stomach wall, and who knows where else. I had had no visible evidence of bleeding and was unaware I had any such problem. The docs felt that slow blood loss had been going on for a long time. I was taken off aspirin and warfarin for a few months. But whatever we did, I continually felt listless, low energy, unable to sustain attention.

Eventually I was referred to a gastroenterologist. I took a friend with me to make notes on questions and answers. Afterward, we both agreed that we'd never seen a less communicative doctor, ever. He booked me for an endoscopy and a colonoscopy at his surgery center (with no explanation of the purposes of each procedure) and sent along papers for me to sign. One form listed rights and responsibilities, which included a statement that resident physicians have ownership interests in their facilities. Another responsibility instructed me to read their policy on Advance Directives. In bold print, it said I was required by federal regulations (which ones?) to sign that document and to bring it with me. I carefully read anything I'm asked to sign. Signing means I agree with it. My alarm bells started going off.

Flip side of the form tells me they do not honor Advance Directives and that they are not required to under the 1990 Patient Self-Determination Act (PSDA). Now, in bold type: **Health care providers...are bound to do all in their power to assure the safe recovery of every patient, including resuscitation if that becomes necessary.** *That knocked out my POLST which says Do Not Resuscitate. I'd invested a lot of heart and research into this matter and here they wanted to disregard it, period. Trust was disintegrating. I talked with the doctor about possible flexibility on this point. The answer was "No." So I canceled the appointments and restarted my research—which helped me settle down.*

I had been living for years with the understanding that the Patient Self Determination Act (PSDA) covered hospitals. Right. I thought surgery was done only inside hospitals. Wrong. PSDA covers hospitals, nursing homes, providers of Medicare-certified hospice programs. No mention of surgical centers, ambulatory or otherwise. They're not exempted by name—they just aren't mentioned in the PSDA. This was verified every place I checked. I wasn't alone in my misunderstanding of the law. I spoke to nurses, medical ethicists, you name it. None knew of this exception—except other surgical centers.

Twice they called me to reschedule; twice I refused. I made an appointment with the hospital doctor who did the earlier endoscopy. He said I didn't need another endoscopy so soon, referring to the pictures he had taken previously. Given my history, he thought a barium enema would be just as useful as a colonoscopy. So that's what we did. (Later, I noticed I hadn't asked what we expected to learn from each procedure. I had gone on old automatic nice-girl obedience to the big-man doctor: "Do what you're told.")

Online, I researched the cost of a barium enema compared to a colonoscopy. The closest I could find for what doctors get paid was "costs without insurance." Barium enemas ranged between $200 and $2,000; colonoscopies between $2,010 and $3,764. (These data may be wildly distorted. Get-

ting actual fee information is most difficult, and they vary considerably, both close to home as well as across the country.)

I speculated, "Could doctor ownership in a surgical center be a motivation to over-prescribe?" Not impossible. Endoscopies and colonoscopies can be "cash cows" for that specialty, I'm told. (But this surgery center has a highly respected reputation, I told myself.) Before my scheduled appointment, my hospital doctor clarified that resuscitation could mean many things such as airway support, not just chest pumping. He sent me a written report of our discussion and decision. This is one excellent example of Informed Consent. My concerns were respected, discussed and recorded before treatment.

I trusted this doctor to give me good care—and I think I got it.

But that wasn't the end. When I get on a medical ethics issue like this, I'm apt to chase it down like a dog with a bone. DNR orders don't have to be respected during a surgical procedure? How can that be ethical? If my Advance Directives and my POLST can be set aside, what about my right to have my decisions respected and acted upon?

HOW CAN ADVANCE DIRECTIVES BE SUSPENDED BY SURGERY CENTERS?

I was surprised to discover that this issue has been widely dealt with in several different professional journals. Here's what the American College of Surgeons (ACS) published in 1994:

> It is generally expected that the surgeon will accept primary responsibility for advising patients regarding risks and benefits when discussing a potential operation. DNR orders…are being used with increasing frequency…so it is even more important that the surgeon take a leadership role in assisting the patient and surgical team through this important aspect of surgical care… [when] the DNR status of such patients during the operative procedure and during immediate postoperative period may need to be modified prior to operation.[15]

It's a short period of time they speak of, but it may be the riskiest time during the entire surgical procedure.

ACS pointed out that "An institutional policy of automatic cancellation of the DNR status…removes the patient from appropriate participation in decision making." They recommended: "A policy of 'required reconsideration' of previous advance directives…. The result of such discussions should be documented in the patient's medical record."[16]

A key factor here would be the different definitions of "resuscitation." If the ambulance arrives and the POLST says to give CPR, that kind of chest-pumping is a radically different kind of resuscitation from supplying airway support during a critical time in a surgical procedure. Again, have a talk with the physician and get the correct language put in your medical record. Then both of you are reasonably protected.

Why bother telling you all this? It's my caution to you when you're asked to sign papers. A hospital nurse told me that patients almost always sign papers put under their noses without reading them. At a critical point in my earlier life, I landed in a "rest home." When a Nurse Ratched type presented me with electroshock papers to sign, I got a jolt in my head that warned, *"Never sign anything you haven't read or don't agree with."* I refused to sign and I got no shock treatments. It saved me from getting my brains fried and gave me personal power I never forgot.

OTHER UNEXPECTED EVENTS: IATROGENIC DISEASES

These are diseases caused by errors in medical treatments or in hospital practices. In 2000 Dr. Barbara Starfield reported about 250,000 deaths a year from these causes:

- 106,000 Non-error, negative effects of drugs
- 80,000 Infections in hospitals
- 45,000 Other errors in hospitals
- 12,000 Unnecessary surgeries
- 7,000 Medication errors in hospitals[17]

These errors are not counted in the Center for Disease Control's death statistics. But if they were, they would be the third most fatal disease in the U.S., after heart disease and cancer. The issue hit big news when the Institute of Medicine published *To Err is Human* in 1999, which detailed these problems extensively.[18] It makes you realize that you could have an emergency in your own hospital. Many hospitals now publish their continuing improvements on a regular basis. However, few report deaths.

The first, simplest, and perhaps most effective change to come about is the hand-washing and gloving that all hospital staff do repeatedly. This substantially reduces the spread of infections and is easy for you, the patient, to see. Watch for reports of other measures being taken. Error reduction in hospitals has become a high priority.

A few exceptional people are working on system-wide changes to reduce errors. One is Dr. Atul Gawande, who wrote *The Checklist Manifesto: How to Get Things Right* in 2010.[19] He visited large systems like Boeing Corporation in Seattle, to study how they reduce errors. Master Builder, an architectural firm, had other kinds of errors to manage or eliminate. Both companies created their specialized checklists and improved essential communications to effectively reduce errors. He also got information from Walmart, the Katrina disaster, and a favorite restaurant in Boston. Checklists tailored to identify their errors plus better interpersonal communications continued to reduce errors.

He then developed ways to apply these observations to surgery procedures. For example, when he formed a new surgery team, they introduced themselves and their roles before the procedure began. This established their identity and function in the team. It reduced negative effects of status within the group—each had a recognized place and value on the team.[19] This may seem obvious, but if your medical team has always been headed by the lead surgeon with a cluster of unidentified "flunkies," these introductions bring identity to all players.

Emergency rooms were kept busy receiving falls and these other injuries. Falls are exceptional. We can be vulnerable a long time.

This chart is just part of nationwide figures collected occasionally by the Center for Disease Control (CDC). All events are marked Unintentional and are treated in hospital emergency departments.

LEADING CAUSE OF NON-FATAL INJURIES IN U.S., 2013					
Rank	25–34	35–44	45–54	55–64	65+
1	Falls	Falls	Falls	Falls	Falls
2	Over Exertion	Over Exertion	Over Exertion	Over Exertion	Struck By/ Against
3	Struck By/ Against	Struck By/ Against	Struck By/ Against	Struck By/ Against	Over Exertion
4	MV Occupant	MV Occupant	Other Specified	MV Occupant	MV Occupant
5	Cut/Pierce	Other Specified	MV Occupant	Other Specified	Cut/Pierce

Falls = from age 25 up, Falls top the list of non-fatal injuries, not just the over-65 crowd.

Struck By/Against refers to fighting or striking out, as in sports.

Overexertion = strain sprains, sports injuries. Too strenuous exercise.

MV-Occupant = motor vehicle passenger/driver gets banged up.

Cut/Pierce = serious accidental cuts, use of hypodermic needles.

Other Specified = injury associated with any other specified cause that does not fit another category. Some examples include causes such as electric current, explosive blast, fireworks, overexposure to radiation, welding flash burn, or animal scratch.

DEATH BY DISEASE BECOMES OUR LAST UNEXPECTED EVENT

Death is that final emergency and death by disease becomes our last unexpected event. Check out this information released by the Center for Disease Control in

2013. It gives the causes of death by age groups. Notice how suicide, homicide and unintentional injury quickly drop off the top five causes. But fast rising as we age are Heart Disease, Malignant Neoplasm, Chronic Low Respiratory and Cerebrovascular. Translation: Heart Disease, Cancer, Lung Disease and Stroke. These data can give you some idea of events yet to come.

LEADING CAUSES OF DEATH BY AGE GROUP IN U.S., 2013					
Rank	25–34	35–44	45–54	55–64	65+
1	Unintentional Injury	Unintentional Injury	Cancer	Cancer	Heart Disease
2	Suicide	Cancer	Heart Disease	Heart Disease	Cancer
3	Homicide	Heart Disease	Unintentional Injury	Unintentional Injury	Lung Disease
4	Cancer	Suicide	Liver Disease	Lung Disease	Stroke
5	Heart Disease	Homicide	Suicide	Diabetes	Alzheimer's Disease

I really don't want some disease to define my end-of-life. I just want to call it "old age." That's easier to accept—I am old. Never mind the health problems that did me in. I'm plain old, and I can accept that I've had my turn at life. Time to move on.

So we've come to a point where we look toward turning terminal. Unexpected events often give us a preview of what comes next. When you're young enough, dying isn't on your to-do list. Once you get past 60 (or whatever age you choose) you may begin to realize that one day you will face the last day of this life. With a bit more information, you can learn a lot about how to make that time easier, whenever it comes. You might plan your "Best Day Possible," and then let go. You may be the first generation wise enough and flexible enough to actually do that.

CHAPTER FOUR

TURNING TERMINAL

Death is a great motivator. You have to get out there and do stuff,
because some day you won't be here.
Of all the advice I've received, I rely on that the most.
– Steve Jobs

- **What Does "Terminal" Mean—Why Is It Important?**
- **How We Disempower Disabled and Paralyzed Persons**
- **Patterns of How We Die**
- **Two Turning Points: Hospice and Hastening Death**
- **Seven Legal Ways You Can Choose to Die**
- ***To Choose to Die: One Man's Experience***

Consider this personal experience excerpted from Dr. Sidney Wanzer's book, *To Die Well.*

"*What do you mean my mother has had a pacemaker installed to keep her alive?*" *I asked, aghast at the news. My ninety-two-year-old mother had severe Alzheimer's disease and for years had been imprisoned in an undignified, meaningless existence.*

"*She developed a dangerous arrhythmia and would not have survived without it,*" *her physician responded.*

"But her living will expressly said she didn't want invasive medical procedures!"

... *"How could you have violated her wishes?!"* *...My mother's living will, written long before she lost her mental faculties, made it clear she did not want her dying senselessly prolonged. Installing a pacemaker in this defenseless, ninety-two-year-old woman was nothing short of a massive medical assault.*

...All her life my mother was a fiercely independent, intellectually vigorous woman used to making her own decisions....

One of Mother's more outspoken, well-known opinions was that she did not want her death prolonged if she became physically or mentally disabled and could no longer lead a meaningful, satisfying life. Many times over the years she proclaimed, "If I ever become senile, just take me out and shoot me." In the 1970s, when living wills first came into use, she signed one, clearly indicating she did not want her death prolonged by medical treatment if the quality of her life ever became so poor that there was no significant intellectual activity....

In 1985, when Mother was ninety years old, she fell getting out of bed and suffered a compression fracture of the spine.... [Eventually, she was admitted to a nursing home.]

...We made sure that her wish not to prolong her death with aggressive medical treatments was prominently displayed in her medical record at the nursing home. Each time I went to visit her I spoke with the head nurse, reminding her of the situation. We gave her doctor a copy of Mother's living will and discussed it with him on several occasions. There seemed to be no chance that her life would be inappropriately extended.

...My Mother lived an additional five years in a helpless, debilitated state lacking all dignity, totally contrary to her written request. During those five years she had no quality of life left....[1]

What went wrong? Again, in Dr. Wanzer's words: "We made one big mistake. We did not ask her doctor explicitly, 'Do you agree with this approach and will you promise to adhere to our mother's wishes?' He had simply listened to us, and we had erroneously assumed that he agreed."[2]

Why didn't they just remove or disable her pacemaker? I wondered.

Dr. Wanzer states, "Nothing could undo the medical travesty that had been visited upon her."[3]

Why not? I wondered, and queried him. While waiting for a response, I wrote the reasoning that I, a writer without legal training, thought should prevail: you have the power to withhold or withdraw life-sustaining treatments, provided it is so stated in your Advance Directive when you were competent, which his mother had done. Why not use it?

It turns out it's not quite so simple. As Dr. Wanzer explained to me in his response, "Removing or disabling the pacemaker in my mother...theoretically might have been carried out on a competent patient who initiated the request himself. However, in an incompetent patient it would expose the physician or family to possible charges of murder—both then and now."

I wanted to understand how implementation of any new law works, so I asked David Kuettel, a California lawyer, to explain how enforcement of a new law develops. Here's what he said: "When a statute is just passed and signed into law, there is no case law interpreting it and thus creates uncertainty as to what extent it requires what action.... It may be a hesitancy on the doctor's part to take action that arguably is permitted under the statute that previously would have constituted a crime (in this case, of murder), without some case law stating there is no liability for acting in accordance with the new statute." Now I understood why Dr. Wanzer couldn't have done other than what he did.

So far, in writing this book, I have talked with you about experiences that I have gone through personally. But I haven't died yet, so what follows is mostly from others' experiences and writings—as seen through my lens on life and death. And it gets down to the nitty gritty of dying.

WHAT'S THE DIFFERENCE BETWEEN HAVING A TERMINAL CONDITION AND BEING DECLARED "TERMINAL"?

Being labeled Terminal is a critical point in the progress of the one or more chronic diseases you may have. It means your physician thinks you are likely to die of your underlying chronic disease within six months. In some situations, the length of time is one year. But if Medicare/Medicaid is paying, they want a six-month limit.

On the other hand, if you have a terminal disease, such as cancer or heart disease, that means you are likely to die from that cause sometime in the future. The prognosis does not include a time limit. This situation is particularly troublesome with some diseases, like Alzheimer's or Persistent Vegetative State, which can go on for years.

So what does this mean for you? Being declared Terminal is a critical decision point. Sometime in the ensuing six months, you can decide to leave acute care—including the ICU—and opt for hospice. You understand that acute care may extend your life but not necessarily improve it—or it may leave you worse off. When you accept that your end is near, that you've had all the medical treatments you can tolerate, and you feel ready to go when your body finally gives out, you may be ready for the change of goals and relief that hospice offers. Most hospice care takes place at home, but is also offered in group homes and similar facilities. One unexpected result happens with some frequency. As you relax and focus on being comfortable in hospice, you may breathe easier and might even live a little longer than you thought you would.

On the other hand, there are people who feel exhausted but are not ready for hospice—they think of hospice as "giving up." They still want all the acute care that the ICU and other hospital resources have to offer even if others, especially their doctors, think it's a losing game. But hospice is not that final. Medicare requires you to sign a statement that you are choosing hospice instead of acute care for your terminal illness. But if you don't die in those six months and you're still terminal, you can have another benefit period of six months—more than once if you live so long. And you have the right to cancel hospice care at any time and return to regular Medicare. Your choices remain open, and you retain some control over your care—a most fortunate arrangement.

The final decision to move from acute to hospice care is yours—assuming you can still make that decision and have the resources to support it. If you can't, this is one more critical issue you need to have talked over with your Agent so that person can speak your deepest desires for you.

But what if you want to go on living and others think your condition isn't worth it? How do disabled or paralyzed people deal with this issue?

HOW DO WE DISEMPOWER DISABLED OR PARALYZED PEOPLE?

Recently, I received an article that gave me great pause. It has to do with the dominant mindset that many health professionals—and myself—have about the worth of a life burdened with serious disabilities. You may have noted in my Health Care Directive that my goal of wanting to remain functional in community assumes that I have a functional body. To be blind, unable to walk or talk, or to have some disease that keeps me bedridden and dependent are conditions that would make life not worthwhile to me. That view seems rational in my present state of unusually good functional health at my ripe old age. But I realize I have projected this view on anyone with disabilities—afflictions I probably will never have to deal with.

William J. Peace, writes in his own voice in "Comfort Care as Denial of Personhood."[4] He's experiencing vomiting that won't stop. He suffers from MRSA—methicillin-resistant *staphylococcus aureus*—a dreaded disease cast onto the public awareness in recent years. Mr. Peace was paralyzed in 1978 and just recently had a "bloody debridement" of a Stage IV wound. That is cleaning out an infected wound that has chewed through all layers of the skin down to clearly visible bone—a most serious condition, especially for a paralyzed person. It's so infectious that caregivers must put on full gowns upon entering the hospital room. Treatment is with certain antibiotics, some of which become useless with time.

The nurse left to get a medication, leaving Mr. Peace in the hands of the hospitalist. She spelled out the gravity of his condition, which he already knew. He would be bedbound for at least six months or a year. There was a good chance the wound would never heal and if so, he couldn't use a wheelchair again—a life of complete dependence. Medical expenses would be staggering, bankruptcy was likely, insurance would run out and life would end in a nursing home. But that wasn't enough. The hospitalist warned that the powerful antibiotics could cause organ damage, his kidneys or liver could fail at any time—wrapping up with the news that MRSA was a life-threatening infection and that many paralyzed people die from such a wound. In other words, he was not Terminal (with no prediction of less-than-six-months of life left), but had a terminal condition that could kill him any day.

The unspoken message was clear: "You're better off dead." I wondered, "Why would anyone want to live that way?" I assumed that my choices, strongly held, would apply to another person whom I don't even know—a personal violation of that person's right to make his own decisions based on his own strongly held choices. And I am not the only one inflicting such a violation on Mr. Peace's rights.

He reports the Office of Protection and Advocacy for Persons with Disabilities found that people with disabilities are sometimes treated as if they were Terminal—starting Do Not Resuscitate orders, withholding or withdrawing nutrition and hydration, withholding or withdrawing medication or pursuing other procedures that would end a life. Presumptions about the quality of their lives were being made for them by medical providers. Mr. Peace sees this bias and bigotry as "the ultimate insult." As a result, he says he never meets a physician without a proper introduction—to establish his credibility as a human being.

In our culture, if a severely disabled person wants to die, it's seen as the reasonable thing to do. We shake our heads in confusion at those who choose to live. This attitude is a threat to the lives of disabled persons and is something we "abled" persons need to be more aware of. Do you recall the power of saying what procedures you DO or DO NOT want in your Health Care Directive? What if hospital staff decides your decisions are wrong? What if they don't follow your wishes because they think you're in such bad shape you should let go? And what if this is not discussed with you? What if you want very much to live, but a "kind-hearted" doctor implies, off the record, that he can help relieve your suffering? Not only is that illegal—it's discriminatory against persons with disabilities who choose to live. What protections are in place for Mr. Peace and others like him?

Under current law, the only option available is to be removed to another facility where other physicians will honor your Advance Directives and your day-to-day decisions—yours or your Agent's. From his experience, Mr. Peace has learned that his disabled body is not considered normal—that the presence of a disabled body creates havoc in a system equipped to deal only with normal bodies.

Another experience comes from Harriet McBryde Johnson, who wrote *Too Late to Die Young: Nearly True Tales from a Life*.[5] Disabled from birth with multiple sclerosis, she gives you a rollicking ride in her wheelchair, protesting and politicking, and generally powering her way through obstacles we "abled" folk unknowingly set up.

The person inside a disabled body has the same rights as the person inside a normal body. For me, having a normal body among the vast majority of other normal bodies has led me to make unconscious assumptions about all persons, including the disabled, which are not true. Mr. Peace's choices about medical treatment must have the same respect as mine—by me as well as the medical system. We must listen—and act according to *their* choices. We must accept their legal and ethical right to live a hard life that I might not choose, but which they may. Each life is a gift. Their choices must be honored, even when we don't understand their love of the only life they know.

That's my opinion. What's yours?

THERE ARE PATTERNS IN HOW WE DIE

Even with extensive medical knowledge, the time and manner of life's end remains capricious and unpredictable. Doctors work from statistical studies, research data, your medical record, their experience—and hunch. They see patterns, and the best they can do is offer predictions—often in the form of percentages or odds—which are based on past experiences of other people.

One way to inform yourself is to consider the trajectories of three eventually fatal chronic illnesses that might happen to you. Lynn and Adamson chart these patterns in *Living Well at the End of Life: Adapting Health Care to Serious Chronic Illness in Old Age*. They summarize "Mostly cancer" cases, "Mostly heart and lung failure," and "Mostly frailty and dementia" cases.[6]

In the SHORT PERIOD OF EVIDENT DECLINE, most patients facing progressive cancer want to slow the cancer's progress and often have good functioning until very late in that pattern.

The second trajectory, LONG TERM LIMITATIONS WITH INTERMITTENT SERIOUS EPISODES, is typical of organ system failure—heart, lungs, liver, and/or kidney conditions. With me, I have had a heart attack and recovered, two bouts of atrial fibrillation, then recovered—but each time not as completely as before. This may happen several times and then, wham, the end comes abruptly. It's hard to plan ahead with this pattern.

The third situation, PROLONGED DWINDLING, applies mostly to frail elderlies and people with Alzheimer's disease or other forms of dementia. Frail folks often have falls or other events that take them out. For people with dementia, it just goes on

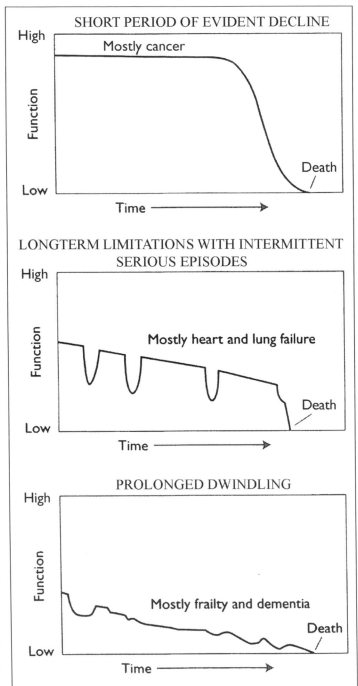

and on, seemingly never-ending, especially for caregivers. According to Joanne Lynn, "…medical people do not generally classify someone as 'dying' from dementia, Parkinson's disease, or just the multiple limitations of advanced old age."[7]

In fact, it has not been possible to die from "old age" since the 1850s when old age was officially medicalized by the World Health Organization (WHO). They set up a data collection system called the International Classification of Diseases (ICD) for monitoring death patterns world wide, which required a standardization of data. Old age was seen as a condition of aging but not a cause of death. As a result, you have to die of one of those 113 causes or your death certificate bounces back to your doctor for conformity. Even if you die of old age, they have to find another way for you to die officially.

Not being labeled Terminal leaves you without eligibility for certain kinds of Medicare help. As the diseases progress, you may not be homebound, so can't qualify for Medicare's home care benefits. To add insult to injury, when you arrive at final stages of your disease, you may not need skilled nursing, but require lots of personal care—which Medicare does not cover if you're not expected to improve. And Alzheimer cases can live a long time. Not fun.

So patterns based on good research and reporting can help, but you can see how difficult it is for physicians to predict when you'll die. Of course if you bring it up you may push your doctor into action. It may be daunting for your doctor to have this talk with you, especially if it's your first serious confrontation with your mortality. No one looks forward to bearing that news unless you've been through so much that you'd be relieved, finally, to get relief. And what if you're so dysfunctional—like being in PVS for a long time—that your Agent must decide all critical issues on your behalf?

And then there's the Zone of Indistinction I mentioned before—that specialized unit outside of the mainstream hospital bustle, where your body can be taken care of when your brain isn't functioning much, but the rest of your body appears to be working, as in a Persistent Vegetative State. Certain bodily functions continue and you may have reflex gestures that suggest you're in there somewhere—like Terri Schiavo who was in such a Zone for 15 years while lawsuits raged.

It's not hard to get there. Sharon R. Kaufman cites one report published in the New England Medical Journal in 1994 that estimated some 35,000 people were in the Zone—25,000 adults and 10,000 children.[8] In March, 2012, the Brain Injury Association estimated about 40,000 people are in a PVS.[9]

I'm not interested in potential PVS for myself. So I use my detailed Health Care Directive, linked to a strong Durable Power of Attorney for Health Care, to prevent this from happening to me (or if it does, my choices provide a legal way out).

One big risk is connected with the use of CPR. As we saw in Chapter 3 which deals with unexpected events, if you have over 4 to 6 minutes without breathing, the risk of brain damage from lack of oxygen is high. Serious brain damage underlies PVS conditions. While Life-Sustaining Treatments are a blessing in many ways, they can also be a curse. Are these treatments sustaining life—or prolonging death? Or maybe we need to revisit more basic issues: what is life—and what is death? When does life end and death begin? Is there a gap—or overlap? There seem to be few tangible lines in the sand.

BUT THERE ARE TWO TURNING POINTS: HOSPICE AND HASTENING DEATH

The first turning point is to choose comfort care. This junction comes when your condition has progressed so far there is no reasonable expectation of a cure or of restoring health. You recognize you are starting to die. Usually people are so exhausted with acute care that doesn't last, or have become so weary of trying to keep an old body performing like its younger version that they become ready to let go. Teamed with your physician, the decision to stop aggressive treatment is the first essential step of comfort care, which is to assist you—and your caregiving family—through the dying process with as much comfort as possible. This decision means that you change your goals from "do whatever it takes" in the ICU to "make me comfortable." Most hospice takes place at home where you're most likely to be comfortable. It can also take place at a hospice center, hospital, or nursing facility—and reduce the amount of family caregiving.

This is the time to have a consultation with your doctor who can outline new medical instructions to support your changed goal. Pain management is often a primary interest, but a whole bundle of actions go into the hospice plan. A general outline that Dr. Wanzer worked up for one of his patients is an example of a starting point.

1. No transfusions.
2. No CPR or other resuscitative measures.
3. No antibiotics for any reason.
4. No intravenous fluids, except to sedate or deliver pain-relieving treatments.
5. If dehydration occurs, no fluids unless you ask for it without urging.
6. No nasogastric tube (no tube feeding).
7. Severe pain to be treated to bring relief, even if it hastens death. If this doesn't work, use stronger drugs, such as morphine. Forget about addiction.
8. No chemotherapy.
9. No transfer to hospital unless essential for symptom control.
10. You are not expected to get out of bed or sit up, unless you want to.
11. No lab tests, x-rays or vital signs should be done.[10]

You could also add no major surgery as well as other limits you want to set.

Putting it all together, you are removing yourself from Life-Sustaining Treatments so you can die naturally. You and your doctor may agree to these things (modified to fit your case), but they must also be carried out by all other nurses and caregivers who help you on your chosen path. You are "letting go" of prolonging your life (of thinking you can live forever) and switching to your chosen comfort care. This change may be difficult for health care workers who are deeply trained to do everything to "save lives" (for how long, with how much pain for you, and at what cost?) The point is to assist you in dying in your own rhythm and comfort. The fight is over—you are accepting what your body is telling you. You regain some control, you breathe easier and can now think about the relief that is in reach. You're becoming ready to finish your family life with all its wonderfulness—and complications.

Now that sounds rather peaceful, even if tough to face. However, it seldom is so simple. Let me share with you a story, written by Doctor Ken Murray, about his view of the picture.

One of my patients was a man named Jack, a 78-year-old who had been ill for years and undergone about 15 major surgical procedures. He explained to me that he never, under any circumstances, wanted to be placed on life support machines again. On Saturday, however, Jack suffered a massive stroke and got admitted to the emergency room unconscious, without his wife. Doctors did everything to resuscitate him and put him on life support in the ICU. This was Jack's worst nightmare. When I arrived at the hospital and took over Jack's care, I spoke to his wife and to hospital staff about his care preferences. Then I turned off the life support machines and sat with him. He died two hours later.

Although he had thoroughly documented his wishes, Jack hadn't died as he'd hoped. The system had intervened. One of the nurses, I later found out, even reported my actions as a possible homicide. Nothing came of it, of course; Jack's wishes had been spelled out explicitly, and he'd left the paperwork to prove it.

But the prospect of a police investigation is terrifying for any physician. I could far more easily have left Jack on life support, prolonging his life and his suffering a few more weeks. I would even have made a little more money, and Medicare would have ended up with an additional $500,000 bill. It's no wonder many doctors err on the side of overtreatment.

But doctors still don't overtreat themselves. Almost anyone can find a way to die in peace at home, and pain can be managed better than ever. Hospice care...provides most people with much better final days... [And he adds]...people placed in hospice care often live longer than people seeking active cures.[11]

How do you know when you are dying and moving into Active Dying? There is a preactive phase which may last about two weeks. According to Dr. Wanzer, you're actively on your way when you start having a cluster of preactive symptoms, such as:

- Increased restlessness, extreme agitation, constantly changing positions.

- Withdrawing from participating in social activities.

- Increased periods of sleep or lethargy.

- Decreased intake of food and liquids.

- Pausing in breathing—apnea—whether awake or asleep.

- Inability to heal or recover from wounds or infections.

- Increased swelling—edema—of extremities, or entire body.

- Wanting to finish "unfinished business," awareness of dying happening.[12]

Active Dying is a progressed cluster of symptoms—you may go in and out of consciousness for three days to two weeks, more or less. According to the Empowering Caregivers website, ways to recognize this stage are:

- Difficulty in arousal, then returning to severely unresponsive state.

- Much longer pauses in breathing, changes in breathing patterns, fast or slow.

- Severe respiratory congestion or fluid buildup in lungs.

- Inability to swallow any fluids or eat any foods at all.

- Breathing with mouth wide open, unable to speak even when awake.

- Blood pressure drops dramatically—more than 20 or 30 points, below 70/50.

- Hands and arms, feet and legs are very cold to touch. Numb, no feeling.

- Cyanosis, or blue or purple coloring in extremities.[13]

All the generalizations made above may happen intermittently, unpredictably, without warning, or not at all, according to Dr. Ann Cutcher, director of Enso House, an end-of-life care home. "No two deaths are ever alike," she says, nodding her head in wonder. "Each one is different, special to that person."

The second turning point is to hasten death, and I can share seven legal ways to do it. When the suffering has become so wearisome, endless and useless, some people will ask their physicians to hasten the dying process. Most physicians are reluctant to get involved personally—they see this action as opposed to the Hippocratic Oath they have taken. Many laws now say doctors should tell you all your options, with the risks and benefits of each, so you can be well informed when you make your final decision. This is what Informed Consent is all about. Occasionally a state will have a law that specifically requires doctors to give you this information, even if the doctor doesn't personally agree with it. Other states, or private hospitals, may have rules against doctors giving you this information. This seems to require physicians to bend the Hippocratic Oath. And they certainly seem to interfere with our right to free speech, depending on where you live, the nature of your illness, or your ability to travel. State laws control. (See Appendix: Hippocratic Oath.)

HERE ARE SEVEN LEGAL WAYS TO HASTEN DEATH

1. Withholding or Withdrawing Life-Sustaining Treatments. The most publicized actions of this method were removing the feeding tubes of Cruzan and Schiavo. The issue of stopping or removing pacemakers has already been discussed. Refusing CPR is another, stopping dialysis would be another. Without certain medical devices to keep you functioning—like a ventilator—you will probably stop living.

2. VSED–Voluntary Stopping Eating and Drinking. Dan Brock explains this in *Physician-Assisted Dying: the Case for Palliative Care and Patient Choice* edited by Timothy E. Quill and Margaret P. Battin. Depending on your condition, this method usually takes from one to three weeks to end your life. It has several advantages. In the final stages of many illnesses, you lose your appetite for eating and drinking anyway. Ethically and legally, you have the right to refuse life-prolonging interventions, including artificial hydration and nutrition. Voluntary refusal of "natural" eating and drinking can be considered an extension of that right. This method protects your privacy and independence and doesn't require any participation by your physician or family.[14]

If you use Dr. Stanley Terman's book called *The Best Way To Say Goodbye: A Legal Peaceful Choice at the End of Life*[15] you'll have the complete story and then some. You will not die of starvation or thirst, although it may look like that to your surviving family. If one could still die of old age, this could be how it happens.

3. Palliative Terminal Sedation. Visualize this scene from Anemona Hartocollis's article in the *New York Times,* "Hard Choice for a Comfortable Death: Sedation":

In almost every room people were sleeping, but not like babies. It was the sleep before—and sometimes until—death. In some of the rooms in the hospice unit at Franklin Hospital in Valley Stream on Long Island, the patients were sleeping because their organs were shutting down, the natural process of death by disease. But at least one patient had been rendered unconscious by strong drugs.

The patient, Leo Oltzik, an 88-year-old man with dementia, congestive heart failure and kidney problems, was brought in by his wife and son who were distressed to see him agitated, jumping out of bed and ripping off his clothes. Now he was sleeping soundly with his mouth wide open.

Mr. Oltzik's life would end not with a bang but with the drip, drip, drip of an IV drug that put him into a slumber from which he would never awaken. That drug, lorazepam, is a strong sedative. Mr. Oltzik was also receiving morphine to kill pain. This combination can slow breathing and heart rate, and may make it impossible for him to eat or drink. In so doing, it can hasten death.

This treatment is palliative sedation—or more starkly—terminal sedation. Doctors who perform it say it is based on carefully thought-out ethical principles in which the goal is never to end someone's life, but only to make the patient more comfortable. The principle is the rule of Double Effect, attributed to 13th century Roman Catholic philosopher Thomas Aquinas. Even if there is a foreseeable bad outcome, like death, it is acceptable if it is unintended and outweighed by an intentional good outcome—the relief of unyielding suffering before death. This is one of the few universal standards on how end-of-life sedation should be carried out.

Mr. Oltzik died after eight days at the hospice. Asked whether the sedation that rendered Mr. Oltzik unconscious could have accelerated his death, Dr. Halbridge said, "I don't know." [15]

4. Helium Hood. Only recently has there been enough detailed information about using helium to end your life in the privacy of your own home. Its originator is Derek Humphry, the founder of the Hemlock Society and author of *Final Exit: The Practicalities of Self-Deliverance and Assisted Suicide for the Dying.*[16] In the third edition, published in 2002, you will find everything you need to know to take this action, including drug information, details of using the hood, questions to ask yourself before doing it, legal forms to complete and communications to leave for family and potential difficulties with police. Whether or not you choose this route, you'll find much useful information here.

This would not be the way I would choose—I can't see myself putting my head in a bag—but two comments of praise for the book could influence my thinking:

From the *American Journal of Law and Medicine:* "An important indictment of medical practice, legal judgment, and the culture at large for failing to find a way to protect people against unwanted suffering and lingering death in the company of strangers.... This book deserves extensive publicity and consideration for what it means to respect people's choices about dying."[17]

From Isaac Asimov: "No decent human being would allow an animal to suffer without putting it out of its misery. It is only to human beings that human beings are so cruel as to allow them to live on in pain, in hopelessness, in living death, without moving a muscle to help them. It is against such attitudes that this book fights."[18]

5. Assisted Dying Abroad: Switzerland and Other Countries. We've heard most about Switzerland's availability of assisted suicide at Dignitas, thanks to a PBS special feature on "Frontline," called "The Suicide Tourist." The patient had ALS *(amyotrophic lateral sclerosis),* better known as "Lou Gehrig's Disease," which is a gradual atrophying of the muscles. It's a progressive disease affecting the whole body; there's no stopping it and it's fatal.

Costs of international travel would have to be added to Dignitas' charges, which the director says are $5,263.16 for preparation and suicide assistance, or $9,210.53 for taking over family duties, including funerals, medical costs and official fees.

More extended worldwide information is found in a Derek Humphry website, *www.assistedsuicide.org/suicide_laws.html* which reviews the state of the art in some 15 countries. Also see *End-of-Life Decision Making: A Cross-National Study* which reports on about a dozen countries, some friendly to the procedure, some not.

6. Old-Fashioned, Traditional Suicide. Under modern U.S. law, suicide is not a crime. Some say attempted suicide is a crime, but it's rarely prosecuted. You might want to check your insurance policy first.

Every once in a while, I hear of some mysterious disappearance, like a tourist cruising in Norway's fjords, not to return. No one knows anything. Odds seem good that this tourist took a dip in the chilly waters, never to rise again. But no one seems to know for sure. It gets forgotten in the crush of current events. Other vanishing acts occur. No one keeps statistics on such things — there's no market. And life goes on.

7. Death with Dignity: Physician Assisted Dying, legal in Oregon and Washington, Montana, Vermont, California and New Mexico. I will probably make this my first choice if I'm eligible. I live in the second state to pass a law allowing it. Washington modeled its law after Oregon's, with follow-through assistance provided by End of Life Washington (formerly Compassion and Choices of Washington). Vermont, California and New Mexico have joined the others, and the campaign to add more states continues. It's controversial, of course.

I wanted to find out more about how the law worked and was fortunate enough to learn about someone who was on that path. I met with Richard three times before he took the potion. The day after, I was able to talk with the three persons who were present at his departure. After absorbing this poignant experience, I wrote an essay of what happened.

> ## TO CHOOSE TO DIE:
> ### One Man's Experience
> ### By Theo Wells
>
> *"Now, I get to decide the day I die."*
>
> *Richard, 96, had just brought home the prescriptions for hastening his death, a process that had taken two months under Washington State's*

Death with Dignity Act. Until now he had felt his terminal cancer would decide the day he would go—and in how much pain.

"Having the prescriptions in hand changes your whole insides," he said. "Now I choose when to go."

Pain was driving his life these days. "Everything else has already happened,"

Richard said. "It's too much effort just to keep myself together. I have to kick myself out of a chair to do things. I don't have any strength left. I just fade and fall down and can't get up by myself. I feel like a piece of rope unraveling.

"Besides, life isn't that important anymore," he added. "I know it's the end. And I can't travel anymore." He'd gone on 225 group fishing trips worldwide, 54 of them with his dear friend Joni, after his wife died many years ago. But cancer had ended those trips.

His daily life was now a waiting game—waiting for the excruciating pain to strike again. He enjoyed the many comforts of living alone as long as his caregiver, Deborah, shopped, cleaned, and cooked for him. He still handled his own finances, and had long since drawn up his end-of-life papers. Living independently and making his own decisions had been his way of life for years.

Now, except for the pain—and aging—life was simple. Twice daily he phoned Joni who lived an hour away. Most of his immediate family had distanced themselves, but they kept in touch.

"I do better with non-family," Richard said.

Each day was a careful balancing act between survival and recurring pain. What day, in what way, would it become too much?

Deborah had worked for Richard only four months, but long enough to become close. She usually came for two hours in the morning, returning in the evening to fix and share dinner. They had developed little rit-

uals, like sharing two after-dinner chocolates, no more, no less. After some TV or reading, he would call Joni for a goodnight chat. Before leaving, Deborah would set his heating blanket at 9-10 and put fresh water by his bed.

One February morning Deborah arrived ten minutes late. It was snowing.

Richard's usual cheery greeting was silent. She found him slumped in his favorite living room chair.

"It's not so good today," he said. "Before you came, I fell." He had tried to unlock the back door. "I can't even get to the back door without falling," he complained.

Deborah had worked with him on how to fall safely and get up again by himself. That day he had painfully managed to get up off the floor and somehow climb back into his favorite chair.

Now he pointed to mid-torso pain traveling through his body. Deborah got him a pain pill and managed to get him to the dining table. But before she could bring breakfast he had a dizzy feeling of a blackout coming on. But it slowly eased.

So Deborah served a breakfast of fresh blueberries and warm oatmeal, sitting along side him in case he choked. He hadn't eaten much when, suddenly, one on top of another, he had six agonizing attacks, cramping his lungs.

Richard decided, "Today's the day I'm taking my meds."

Deborah stood with him. "Whatever you choose, I'm helping."

First, Richard called Joni and arranged for her and her husband, Joseph, to come as witnesses. Next he notified his son who was vacationing in Hawaii. Then he asked two of his grandsons in their thirties, who lived nearby, to come over.

The grandsons arrived promptly, happy to see him one last time. Their father had called from Hawaii, sending the message, "I wish you all a peaceful day."

They reminisced some about their family relations being 'different,' when Richard cleared his throat, his signal for them to go home.

Half an hour later, Joni and Joseph arrived. Now preparations for the final event could begin. Settling in with cups of coffee, they all reviewed the instructions with Deborah, which she and Richard had rehearsed several times. It would take about thirty minutes to empty the many barbiturate capsules, mix and dissolve them in water. Richard, unaided, had to down it in two gulps, and it would be foul-tasting.

Now was the time for Richard to take the two meds to prevent nausea and vomiting. Thirty to sixty minutes later he would take the final draught.

To give Richard and Joni some alone time, Deborah and Joseph went to the kitchen. Deborah worked steadily, emptying and dissolving the powder in a highball glass, while Joseph stood around recalling fishing stories.

"It's ready," Deborah said, taking the mixture to the living room.

Then all four went to Richard's bedroom and Deborah got him settled on his red down comforter. He took the glass. As if toasting them, they shared a few last words. Murmurs of "I love you" circled the bed.

Richard downed the mixture in two large gulps at 2:05 in the afternoon. It was Deborah's job to record such details. Then they waited, Deborah holding his left hand, Joni his right, and Joseph, his toes. Full attention was glued on Richard. His eyes were still open. About two minutes later, he said, "I thought this was supposed to work fast."

"Be patient." Deborah stayed calm.

Thirty seconds later, Richard noted, "Didn't taste too bad either."

Deborah took his wrist, feeling for a pulse. His eyes closed, his pulse slowed, then stopped. The time was 2:12. It had taken just seven minutes. They didn't move, each in their own feelings—a sense of oneness, of letting go, of peace.

What do people do at such a time? They did ordinary things. Joseph washed up the coffee cups. Joni called to stop the newspaper. Deborah documented the time of death, then made the critical call to hospice. They would arrange the declaration of death, call the funeral home and report to the Department of Health. Soon the mortuary called to say they'd pick up the body within two hours.

More waiting. Deborah collected the instructions and prescription information sheets to take home to protect privacy. Joseph collected all remaining medications for Deborah to dispose of safely. Joni went quietly around the house restoring order.

Deborah looked in on Richard one last time. She seemed to feel an "energy" coming from him. She knelt by his bed, held his hand and leaned into him, like a mother. "I'll see you next time," was her personal goodbye.

Joni and Joseph then took charge, releasing Deborah with, "You don't have to stay." It had been a long emotional day for her, but now this job was over.

Richard's death certificate would show cancer as the cause of death.

His life ended as he had wanted. He had gotten back his control. His chosen family was there for him to the end.

They loved him enough to let him die.

This is a true story with the names changed. Confidentiality is protected by the law. For Death with Dignity Act details for Washington State, see *www.doh.wa.gov/dwda.*

End of Life Washington provides support and guidance to qualified patients who want to use the Death with Dignity Act. Contact them at 1-877-222-2816 or visit their website at *www.EndofLifeWA.org.*

Turning Terminal is a hard concept to handle. So let's back up and talk about "Turning Patient" and look at what that means. When you bump into your doctor at the grocery store, you're a person. When you walk into her office, you're a patient. Why? You're still you. Or are you?

Think about putting on that blue-dotted sack they hand you, whether you're undressing for a chest X-ray or about to climb into a hospital bed. The system does not provide a closed backside. You do what you're told. You step outside and stand in the hallway, momentarily ignored by bustling staff. Someone comes to your rescue and escorts you to an unknown destination, so you grab the back flaps of your designer gown and try to stand tall. It doesn't work.

Congratulations! You have just "Turned Patient." And what happens to your sense of personal power? How do you keep or regain it in these circumstances?

In the next chapter, we deal with reclaiming your power even when you're bare-assed. If you are going to have your decisions followed, such changes are part of the game.

CHAPTER FIVE

COMMUNICATING TO GET YOUR DECISIONS FOLLOWED

The single biggest problem in communication is the illusion that it has taken place. – *George Bernard Shaw*

- **Start with Your Own Personhood**
- **From Hippocratic Oath to Informed Consent**
- **Medical Mindsets vs. You and Your Agent**
- **How It Can Go So Wrong? The Ruth Adler Case**
- **The Conversation: Talking About Your End-of-Life Care**
- **Take More Control Over Your Own Decisions**

Another trip to the ER. I am ambulanced to the local community hospital with "flash pulmonary edema." Even with oxygen support, I gasp for each breath during the 25-minute ride. Scary. Poor recovery leads to an angio gram to determine next steps. Local hospital isn't equipped for this, so I go to the suburban medical center, newly expanded and refurbished, where my cardiologist performs his magic in architectural splendor. Moving past the 3rd floor admissions desk, I'm greeted with the grandeur of modern medicine—miles of high gloss marble floors, walls of glass windows, spirals— then details fade. I feel like the tired old lady I am. It is big. I am small.

On to an enlarged prep room. Off come the clothes. On goes the gown, only this one is soft pink paper with an odd lining of some sort, full but still leaving me bare-assed until the nurse overlaps the back flaps and carefully fastens a rear strap. Modesty is rescued—a good sign. For the next hour, more or less, I am prepped for running that tiny camera up my big artery:

groin shaved, blood pressure, temperature, clothes-pin on finger, other vitals measured ad nauseum. *It keeps two nurses bustling for almost an hour. As every detail is recorded, I slowly recede into patienthood like fading into a tunnel.*

But before my final evaporation, one last thing saves my humanity. The nurse asks if I would like a warm blanket. Now there's nothing like a little warmth after all that prep in a chilly room, so of course I glom on to that promise of comfort. But I don't get the skimpy warmed blanket that my home-town hospital provides. The nurse fusses a little with the pink gown lining and suddenly, my whole body is suffused in gentle warmth. Surprise! I feel human again, kind of young human, almost cuddly. What is this? A simple device, like a hair dryer, plugged into a warm air supply that gently floats inside the pink gown. Mmmmm.

Just as I am getting used to my rejuvenation, I'm unhooked from my warmth and rolled down halls, into elevators, past nursing stations, to the working inner sanctum. This rotunda has morphed into at least twice the size of the old one—now perhaps 30 x 30 feet with a 20-foot domed ceiling, laced with curving tubes and latticed square cords (for what functions I have no idea). I am shifted onto the central table. All wait expectantly—almost at attention—for the arrival of the gods. My doctor enters.

Flashback to last visit with this doc at my hometown hospital where he holds forth once a month. He is standing, braced against the wall, opposite the chair built for the 300-pound patient—in which I have to slump for-ward for my elbows to reach the armrests—while he perfunctorily answers my questions. No interaction, just back and forth, like ping-pong. Awkward. He's maybe 50 and rather good-looking, I'm 86 and a bit worn around the edges. Does this matter? I hope not.

Flashback to another trip to this specialist—at his home base. Recovery is unexpectedly slow. A friend has come along to take notes, ask questions and record results. I tell her not to be surprised if I get aggressive and insist he sit down and really talk with me. But he surprises us. Comfortable in his own surroundings, he sits and chats like an interested human being, speak-

ing with me as if I have my marbles. I am accepted as an intelligent person capable of making my own decisions. Like partners—sort of.

Now back to the rotunda. He who enters has morphed into an intense, though relaxed, medical expert, first trained on a cadaver. I am sleepy, relaxed, primed to explore his thoughts. My pragmatism says he now sees me as an old, wrinkled body—at least my dentures are in—but do I look like a cadaver to him? His expertise can perform the magic that gives me more breathing time on earth. Like God. He performs, instructs, disappears. Is there a rapid-change sanctuary somewhere in which he morphs back into a human peer? Where I drop my patienthood and become a person again? Where we can look eye-to-eye like partners once more?

Before the day is out I'm prepped to leave and regain my dignity—my personhood—in the outside, profane world. I exit by wheelchair, leaving behind this medical cathedral consecrated to the well-being of humankind. I breathe easier as I leave, thankful to still be breathing.

Question: How can a doctor switch from a person-to-person relationship, to performing doctor-to-patient medical procedures, then revert back to person-to-person when he's finished? And be scheduled for another such procedure before lunch? How do they do it—or do they?

It's much easier to be the person-turned-patient. All I have to do is lie around and be fixed—and pay the bill. (On my "This Is Not a Bill" statement, total charges for time in the rotunda came to $10,072.45. My cardiologist got a mere $836.00. If I were in his shoes, I'd feel shortchanged.)

But back to reclaiming my personhood—to being in control again. It's my body. I get to decide what treatments it receives or refuses. But first the doc has to spell out my options and risks—a different kind of partnership called Informed Consent.

FROM HIPPOCRATIC OATH TO TODAY'S INFORMED CONSENT

Informed Consent is all about your making your own decisions about what treatments you do or don't want performed on your body at any time, especially at end-of-life. It started out rather poorly. Wikipedia summarizes the history of Informed Consent nicely:

500 BCE, in the Greek text the Hippocratic Oath advises physicians to conceal most information from patients in order to give the patients the best care. The doctor knows better than the patient and therefore should direct the patient's care because the patient is not likely to have ideas which would be better than the doctor's.

14th Century, building on the above, Henri de Mondeville, French surgeon, thought doctors should "promise a cure to every patient" in hopes that a good prognosis would inspire a good outcome—like today's positive thinking.

18th Century, Benjamin Rush thought doctors ought to share as much information as possible—that doctors educate the public—but that patients should be strictly obedient to the physician's orders. The ethical principle of beneficence was best done by making decisions for patients without their consent.

1803, Thomas Percival was still a student of the earlier Hippocratic physicians. While he believed patients had a right to the truth, he also believed the physician could provide better treatment by lying or withholding information.

1849, Washington Hooker wrote a radical medical ethics book that advocated rejecting all advice that a doctor should lie to patients. He felt deception was not fair to the patient, but it seems his ideas were not very influential.

Highlights of historical landmark cases that follow are drawn from Dr. Peter M. Murray's article, "The History of Informed Consent."

1914, New York: Schoendorff v. Society of New York Hospital first established that the patient was an active participant in the treatment decision process. Quoting Associate Justice of the U.S. Supreme Court Benjamin Cardozo: "Every human being of adult years and sound mind has a right to determine what shall be done with his own body; and a surgeon who performs an operation without his patient's consent commits a battery for which he is liable in damages."[1]

Then some twenty cases are briefed, slowly building a body of law, many of which deal with details of doctor liability and other considerations needed for valid consent.

1947 brought the Nuremburg Trials which dealt mostly with the effects of German human experimentation during World War II. It established that "the voluntary consent of the human subject is absolutely essential."

1948, the Declaration of Geneva, also influenced by the Nuremburg Trials, was devised and adopted by the World Medical Association only three months before the United Nations General Assembly adopted the Universal Declaration of Human Rights in December of 1948. (See Appendix 3: for the text of a modern version of the *Hippocratic Oath.*)

1972, Washington, D.C.: in Canterbury v. Spence the court outlined requirements for Informed Consent before a surgical procedure, and potential liability if not done.

WHAT IS INFORMED CONSENT AND WHY IS IT IMPORTANT?

Informed Consent is an ethical and legal procedure to be sure that you, the patient, are aware of the potential benefits and risks of a recommended treatment. That's what you need to know in order to decide whether you DO or DO NOT want any of it done. Your physician suggests what she considers to be your best option with its benefits and risks. If you say NO, she'll offer a next best option—if there is one—for you to consider. You should also be told the benefits and risks if nothing is done. This may include information about how numb they can keep your pain, or about how much more time they predict you might live. Then you decide what you DO and DO NOT want done. Your doctor is legally obligated to give you the information, and you are responsible for signing off on the decisions you make based upon that information.

But Informed Consent is more than getting you to sign a written consent form. It is a process of communication between you and your physician that results in your agreement and authorization to undergo a specific medical intervention. In the communication process, your physician should disclose and discuss these points:

- **Your diagnosis, if known.**
- **The nature and purpose of a proposed treatment or procedure.**
- **The risks and benefits of that proposed treatment.**
- **Alternate treatments, if any.**
- **Risks and benefits of each alternative treatment.**
- **Risks and benefits of not receiving any treatment.**

In turn, you should ask questions so you can make an informed YES or NO decision to proceed or not. You also have the right to refuse all treatments if you so choose.

The communication process is both an ethical obligation and a legal requirement spelled out in statutes and case law in all 50 states. Patient autonomy is the overarching ethical consideration that forms the core of Informed Consent. The AMA's Code of Medical Ethics states that physicians must provide relevant information to you. The full disclosure of relevant information is intended to protect your right to self-determination, bodily integrity, and your voluntariness in making these decisions. Providing relevant information to you has long been a physician's ethical obligation, but the legal concept of Informed Consent itself is recent.

Once you or your Agent makes the decision, it should be noted in your medical record *before* the procedure is done. This establishes your authority, your power, to make this decision. You are giving written permission for your doc to act on your decision—*after* you understand what is to be done. Sometimes the doc's office staffers will ask you to sign the Informed Consent form before you see the doctor. Just hang on to it until you are satisfied you have the information you need. Remember—it's your decision, not theirs, that must be recorded.

Outpatient clinics, especially surgery, may try to expedite this paperwork, and you sign whatever they put in front of you for fear they won't do the procedure if you don't. And they probably won't. But what if your wishes differ from what the doctor recommends? Signing a written consent could bring you an outcome you don't want, but which meets the doctor's agenda.

MEDICAL MINDSETS VS. YOU AND YOUR AGENT

Let's start with the traditional relationship between the patient and the doctor.

One day, I was at an opening of a new EMS facility hawking POLST forms since many visitors didn't know about them. I spoke of the importance of writing out certain decisions on these forms in case of an emergency. One woman, let's call her Donna, perhaps in her 70's, cut me dead with: "My doctor makes those kind of decisions for me. I trust him completely." (Sniff.)

And that's the way it always was—in horse-and-buggy country doctor days when he (always a "he") held all medical knowledge and would, if necessary, accept a picked chicken in payment. Patients had no access to what little medical information there was and were almost totally dependent on the doctor. A woman was not used to questioning the instructions of men, especially the revered doctor whom she trusted. But that was in another century. Dr. Arthur E. Hertzler wrote about it in 1938 in his entertaining book, *The Horse and Buggy Doctor*[2]—still in print!

In terms of communication, the rural medicine man was a special kind of god—a benevolent carrier of old and new wisdom. But even as we became more citified, as we gradually made major medical discoveries   followed by the great surge of changes we've already briefed during the last thirty years—reverence for the doctor has generally held. We looked up to him *and her* and usually do so today. We also know much more about taking care of our own health, thanks to access to information not readily available before.

But all those changes did little to change the prevailing medical mindset that grew out of this history. It's best for doctors to speak for themselves, so let me share with you two well-regarded doctors telling us what it's like to be totally committed to their work.

First is the late Sherwin B. Nuland, author of *How We Die: Reflections on Life's Final Chapter* as he worked with Miss Hazel Welch, who was mad at him because he didn't let her die as she wished. He was certain he had done the right thing—she had, after all, survived. Upon reflection though, Dr. Nuland saw things a bit differently.

I had betrayed her by minimizing the difficulties of the postoperative period.... She was obviously one of those people to whom survival was not worth the cost.... I was guilty of the worst sort of paternalism. I had withheld information because I was afraid the patient might use it to make what I thought of as a wrong decision....[3]

In thinking through his actions, he also realized that he was strongly influenced by his surgeon colleagues in their weekly mortality and morbidity (M&M) sessions—a self-presented review to colleagues of deaths that occurred on his watch.

I knew I would probably have done exactly the same thing again, or risk the scorn of my peers.... The code of the profession of surgery demands that no patient as salvageable as Miss Welch be allowed to die if a straightforward operation can save her, and we who would break that fundamental rule, no matter the humaneness of our motive, do so at our own peril.... I can imagine what I might hear: "How could you let her talk you into it?" "Does the mere fact that an old lady wants to die mean that you should be a party to it? ...A surgeon should only make clinical decisions, and the right clinical decision was to operate—leave moralizing to the ministers!" One way or another, the rescue credo of high-tech medicine wins out, as it almost always does.

My treatment of Miss Welch was based not on her goals but on mine, and on the accepted code of my specialty. I pursued a form of futility that deprived her of the particular kind of hope she had longed for—the hope that she could leave this world without interference when an opportunity arose.... Instead, she suffered the fate of so many of today's hospitalized dying, which is to be separated from reality by the very biotechnology and professional standards that are meant to return people to a meaningful life.[4]

But, practically speaking, biotechnology and professional standards still don't include you and me in the decision process. Fourteen years later Dr. Pauline Chen, in her book, *Final Exam: A Surgeon's Reflections on Mortality* says much the same thing: "Death, for surgeons, is immensely and profoundly personal: it is about us. Once death becomes inevitable in surgery, surgeons would hastily do everything possible to close up and rush the patient out of the OR, even if that patient expired only a few minutes later in the ICU. Why? Because a death in the OR means it is the surgeon's fault, and you have to do everything to prevent that.... M&M, our professional ritual centered on death, attempts to heal the rents in our professional fabric caused by patient deaths. There are few other opportunities for surgeons to discuss death....it seeks to transform death's loss into an affirmative experience."[5]

She speaks of another trick of the trade: "I learned how to *turf,* to send difficult, time-consuming problems to someone else.... I knew someone had to tell these patients about the terrible diagnosis...but I knew that if I held off long enough, someone else probably would.... I did not have to lie, and I did not have to divulge the truth.... But the fact that I could not muster the strength to tell the truth to these patients sickened me."[6]

But gradually during training and learning to face the difficult, Dr. Chen found that conversing with patients was *not* a skill that came with practice. In fact, it was only at the end of her training she remembered the potent advice of a lecturer: "You'll be a better doctor if you can stand in your patient's shoes."[7]

That's a profound shift—from doctors thinking the treatment choice is theirs to make, to your deciding jointly with your doctor—given good information. Getting that good information is what Informed Consent is all about.

But in case after case, I read of end-of-life situations where patients or Agents give away—or never pick up—their personal power to decide these issues. I also see how the medics can't seem to let go of thinking the decision is theirs to make—after all, since the 5th BCE, they've known what's best for the patient. Take Ruth Adler's struggle.

HOW IT CAN GO SO WRONG? THE RUTH ADLER CASE

Ruth Adler's case is reported by Doctors Jerome Groopman and Pamela Hartzband in *Your Mechanical Mind; How to Decide What Is Right for You.* Consider several decision points that Ruth Adler, a 75-year-old dying woman had in her last hospital experience. Ten years before, she had already chosen her rabbi, psalms and music for her funeral. At that time, she had fainted from loss of blood due to narrowing of the aortic valve in her heart. The first procedure the doctors recommended was open heart surgery to replace the valve.

Ruth had named her husband as her legal Agent who, like the doctor, was committed to saving her life by whatever means necessary. Her Health Care Directive said she wanted "no heroic measures," but used fuzzy definitions of "temporary or permanent" Life-Sustaining Treatments. Apparently she didn't state much about her values, other than being adamant that she never wanted to go to rehab. She told her daughter, Naomi, that she was tired of all the surgery and never wanted to go to the hospital again.

Here's a summary of occasions when Ruth had to fend off the wishes of her Agent-husband, daughter and doctor—because of their confusion over "who decides."

1. Emergency trip to hospital where she was about to go into shock, Ruth says to doctor: NO. "I do not want any artificial assistance, none at all."

2. She develops sepsis and it is hard for her to breathe. On refusing to go on a ventilator: NO. "I don't want to be a vegetable. I want to be active, or gone."

3. Same as 2. Doctor says ventilator would only be temporary. Again Ruth says NO.

4. Doctor says Ruth will probably die if they don't put her on ventilator. Again: NO. "I don't want to be on a breathing machine, and I don't want to be transferred to a chronic care facility."

5. Nurse to daughter Naomi: "My own father finally agreed to a ventilator and after a few days he was able to come off it." Naomi to Ruth: "Mom, please consider this." PRESSURE.

6. Doctor: "Not more than a few days on the ventilator. Think about it again." PRESSURE.

7. Agent-husband takes short home break. Ruth starts to gasp for breath. Different doctor acts as blood pressure falls: "You need to be intubated now. We need to get you on the ventilator." PRESSURE.

8. Ruth: "I need to think about it. I need five minutes." Doctor: "You may not have five minutes." PRESSURE. Ruth: "I'm not going to be pressured by you. I need to call my husband." Question for Agent-husband: Is a week on a ventilator a "heroic measure"? Ruth couldn't anticipate every event when writing her Advance Directive, but husband and doctor slide over Ruth's fear of Persistent Vegetative State. Doctors believe Ruth could regain an active, healthy life if she'd only agree. PRESSURE.

9. The doctors feel that holding strictly to her Advance Directive is not in her best interests. Yet they cannot treat her without her explicit permission. Ruth gives in and accepts short-term ventilation. PRESSURE.

10. Complications from prior surgery cause infection that antibiotics can't treat. Doctor says two surgeries are required: one, to repair earlier bone damage, two, to close the skin that was burned from earlier cancer radiation. A disease specialist confers with daughter and Agent-husband: "She couldn't beat this, even with surgery." But, a thoracic surgeon evaluates: "We can do this." MORE PRESSURE.

11. Daughter and Agent-husband discuss for two hours. Decision: NO. Reason: they know if Ruth finds out they consented to a surgery she had refused, she'll be angry.

12. Ruth develops atrial fibrillation. Should she have a cardioversion—a shock to get her heart back on rhythm? Daughter and Agent-husband give permission, feeling that a shock is neither "heroic" nor "artificially sustaining" her. But will Ruth see it that way? They realize how specific they have to be to fulfill Ruth's wishes. LEARNING.

13. Discussion: Agent-husband wants daughter to join him in making decisions, although rest of family may not agree with them. But who wants to prolong her suffering? Giving families information doesn't produce consensus. Naomi: "Ultimately, we had to honor my mother's wishes, even though they were not what we wanted." RUTH PREVAILS.

14. Ruth has been intubated for a week since she agreed to the ventilator, when a tube was run through her nose or throat down the windpipe to lungs, to keep an airway open. Naomi: "Everything my mother feared was happening to her." PROBLEM.

15. Doctor removes tube, Ruth reaches out like trying to draw air from the window. Doctor puts an oxygen mask on her, saying: "We may have to put the tube back." Ruth can't speak but shakes her head: NO, NO. She doesn't fight when they reinsert the tube. She awakes to being on the ventilator and is angry. VIOLATION.

16. Doctor: Tube has been in too long and has to be removed. Next step is a tracheotomy, where they make a hole in her neck to insert the tube directly into the trachea. Then they will discharge her to a rehab facility until she can again breathe on her own. Ruth refuses treatment and rehab again. NO.

17. Doctor: "If she can't breathe on her own, she'll need the tracheotomy." Ruth can't breathe on her own and is told she needs the surgery. She shakes her head: NO.

18. Doctor: "If you make that choice, you will die." Ruth, whispering, says NO.

19. Ruth's Agent-husband throws himself on her bed: "Please Ruth, please." Ruth again shakes her head: NO. He did not understand the DPOA-HC role.

20. Daughter, Naomi, stays with her all night so she won't be alone. Then she goes home to freshen up, leaving a request for a call if anything changes. Two minutes before Naomi arrives Ruth dies. Finally, Ruth gets her YES.[8]

What did Ruth's caregivers not understand about NO? We see a combination of Agent-husband and daughter, together with physician's medical mindset, trying to persuade Ruth to change the decisions she had made in her Advance Directive.

Let's guess what the key difficulties here might be.

The Agent arrangement seems fuzzy. Ruth's husband is the designated Agent, but part way through, he tells the doctors that both Naomi and he will make the decisions. That is not his decision to make. Ruth chose him—but we don't know whether or not they understood what that choice might mean. He's supposed to do whatever it takes to make Ruth's health care decisions happen, even if they differ from his personal wishes. But the nearer to death Ruth gets, the more he deviates from her wishes and wants to share those decisions with their daughter. Naomi, not chosen by her mother, goes along with that. It seems there never was mutual agreement about this responsibility, even if they had realized what might be involved. They needed more discussion about her decisions for no CPR, no ventilators, and no rehab—and her values on which these decisions were made. Ruth seems adamant about wanting to avoid PVS. Having one decision-maker at a time becomes vitally important. Physicians often try to get family agreement on final decisions, whether or not the AD is followed. If the Agent-husband wants to confer with family, fine. But the final decision is the Agent's to make when Ruth can't decide. Many doctors and families ignore this fact at the deathbed.

Ruth needed her husband to support her instructions, not sabotage them. Unintentionally, Ruth was violated by those she trusted most.

Forgetting the family's obligation to "walk in Ruth's shoes" is understandable, especially if Ruth didn't discuss her Health Care Directive with them very much. But is it understandable for the medics to ignore them too? Back to that medical mindset physicians develop in the years of med school and specialty training. It's pounded into them. Sherwin Nuland suggested powerful causes: "…of all the professions, medicine is one of the most likely to attract people with high personal anxieties about dying. We become doctors because our ability to cure gives us power over the death of which we are so afraid. Another factor in the personalities of many doctors…a need to control…." [9]

Pauline Chen, in her own words: "That we can fend off disease and death through our actions is an intoxicating notion…. There is no mistaking the heady exhilaration you feel when you walk into the cool and ordered operating room, pull out all the technical gadgetry and wizardry of the moment, and within a few hours solve the essential problem. Surgery is a specialty defined by action." [10]

But there's a deeper idea that has been embedded through medical training that "more treatment equals more love." According to Chen, "Any decision to hold or even withdraw treatment becomes nearly impossible, and not treating a patient becomes the moral equivalent of giving up. Moreover, once a treatment has been started, there is an obligation to the interventions themselves. Having done so much already, doctors—and many patients and families—find it nearly impossible to let all their efforts simply drop. We battle away until the last precious hours of life, believing that cure is the only goal." [11]

In Ruth's view care, not cure, was the only goal. Her goal got lost.

The puzzle of end-of-life decisions is over for Ruth. But not for the family, not for the doctors, not the hospital. Chen found research on this dilemma, where one-third of the physicians and three-quarters of the residents felt they had acted against their conscience in providing care to the terminally ill. "*I mean, how much can you do to a person?*"[12] But they all move on—to repeat it tomorrow.

This leaves unanswered the question: When do physicians, families and patients know when to stop treating and begin palliating? That's when you move out of the ICU and into pain relief and activities that give you and your family comfort and enjoyment as the end nears.

Let's hear from an end-of-life specialist, Dr. Ed Creagan of the Mayo Clinic, who has had a bit of experience with dying folks. He's an advocate for avoiding unnecessary treatment, especially when it's clear there's no benefit. He says, "I have been touched by about 40,000 clinical encounters with the terminally ill. Most of us will spend the last 10 days of our lives with overwhelming pain if there is not a palliative-care specialist present."[13] This is worth preparing for, and it brings us to the Conversation.

THE CONVERSATION—DECIDING ABOUT YOUR END OF LIFE CARE

We've seen examples of how physicians are reluctant to initiate a Conversation that goes against their "save lives" mindset. Who should initiate the Conversation, the doc or you? A number of articles in the professional journals point to the physician as the one responsible to bring it up—rarely you, the patient.

I suggest the initiative should come from you, who will make your end-of-life decisions. No one knows your goals and preferences better than you do. No one—except your Agent—has so much at stake in seeing that your choices are carried out. You are the responsible one. If you can't or don't do it when the time comes, your doctor can start the Conversation, but you need to take responsibility for the decisions—just as Ruth did. But unlike Ruth, you need to talk with family and physicians about your desires and garner their support. If you have a stubborn family member who could gum up the works, you need to name who is *not* to be part of your late-life decision making. You are in charge—or should be. It's your life.

But you can't control everything. "It's almost impossible for patients really to be in charge," says Dr. Joanne Lynn, a physician and director of the nonprofit Altarum Center for Elder Care and Advanced Illness in Washington, D.C. "We enforce a kind of learned helplessness, especially in hospitals." When asked how much unwanted treatment gets delivered, she couldn't come up with a figure, but she said, "It's huge, however you measure it. Especially when people get very, very sick."[14]

It's true that existing systems, like hospitals, clinics and nursing homes, often operate on their own schedules and rules which may not include your Advance Directive. Even though you work closely with them there will be slip-ups you can't control that get results you don't want. Remember Dr. Wanzler's experience, from Chapter 4? But Ruth Adler's nightmare should not happen to you if you do your ongoing homework with your Agent and your family. Ideally, you should go out of this world on your own terms.

A good way of communicating with different mindsets is by using a "YouTube mind." What we see in pictures and live action is more easily understood than the same thing described in writing. The principle is, "Show, don't tell." If I had told you: "Ruth Adler had to fight through twenty pressures to change her mind about how she wanted to end her life," you would have had no internal experience of all she went through. By showing what happened at every turn, you were able to feel the pressures as she did, and your internal experience came alive as it moved from head to heart.

This concept of "showing" is being developed by Angelo Volandes, M.D., an assistant professor at Harvard Medical School who is featured in an *Atlantic* article, "How Not to Die," by Jonathan Rauch. Volandes believes, "There's nothing more essential to being a good doctor than your ability to communicate."[15] He is developing a series of short videos to show risks and benefits of treatments for various diseases. In one he shows a woman with advanced dementia, followed by images to help you understand three options for her medical care. Here, in one brief video, he provides the essential information needed for Informed Consent by her Agent and family caregivers—her options, risks and benefits. In this way they choose treatments most consistent with the wishes this woman stated when she was able to think and speak for herself.

Another version of this idea is used by Honoring Choices Minnesota who developed a great number of two to three-minute videos. These are available at *www. HonoringChoices.org.*

TO TAKE MORE CONTROL OVER YOUR OWN DECISIONS, TAKE MORE CONTROL OF YOUR COMMUNICATION SKILLS

One type of communication is what we see in emotional or conflict situations. We often *react* when we might better stop, listen, think of results we want, choose our best options—then *act*. To do this you have to become aware of your own reacting. For that you might use a technique I developed: the Incident Card.[16]

Stop and write down what happened, what you did, how you felt, and what you want to do next time. Then you'll know what action you want to choose. This puts you in control and soon you'll be able to just stop and ask yourself, "What result do I want?"

Self-control is what it's all about. That and better decisions. You'll be able to move from "Who's to blame?" to "What results do we want?" (Notice it's now "we" wanting results.) You stay in a problem-solving state of mind—and that keeps you acting effectively.

This is a two-way process. You are interacting with another person who may not be thinking as clearly as you. They too have results they want—probably different from yours. If you are determined to get your way, you may listen but *not hear* them. You'll be in Debate mode. Your goal is to outwit them. Good old competition!

On the other hand, if you want to figure out a mutual solution, you will listen and respond in a way that lets others know you are *lis-*

INCIDENT CARD
☐ **I made it**   ☐ **I avoided it**   ☐ **I blew it**
What happened?
What I did was
What my feelings were
What I want to be ready to do next time
So I can feel

tening and *hearing* their viewpoint. You are having a genuine conversation—a Dialogue. That invites them to Debate less and start listening to you for a cue. Now you may have a real possibility of finding ways that get you both some (if not all) of what you want—mutual gain. Here is what that process looks like—practice with your family.

HOW TO LISTEN	
And Not Hear	**And Hear Others**
Debate	**Dialogue**
Listen, then list your rebuttals	Listen, then list *their* rebuttals
Defend your position	Hear *their* position
Give answers	Explore options
Interpret, judge others' behavior as right or wrong	Observe, describe others' behavior without evaluating
Assume you know what they mean	State what you heard, verify
Think either-or, find one best way	Think more-or-less without evaluating
Give advice on what's best	Share ideas and information
Evaluate each other's views	Accept and give your views
Overcome objections	Respect differences
Ask "Why don't you?" questions	Ask "How can we?" questions
Strive to win	Seek mutual gain
Make points now to build your track record	Build relationships to create mutual benefits
Competitive	**Conversational**
Control Status Quo	**Open Up New Options**

As I said in my book, *Keeping Your Cool Under Fire: Communicating Non-Defensively:*

> **When you react, you give away your power—and make nice.**
>
> **When you act, you keep your power—and make decisions.**[17]

Now we come to the nitty-gritty part of Take Care of Dying. First is getting these documents signed, copied, distributed, filed and available for future revision. Once you've done all this work, you have to communicate it—and track who got what, and when. I've devised a simple way to do that. But while you're at it, you may as well organize your end-of-life papers so your Personal Agent or Representative can easily find the documents needed to close your affairs after you've gone on. Not only will that be a service to that person, it will make your present paperwork easier. I have to admit that I'll finish organizing my own papers while I write this chapter. It's still not done—is it ever final before one dies?

CHAPTER SIX

MANAGING YOUR PAPERWORK

Begin at the beginning, keep going until you get to the end, then stop.
—Source unknown

- *When Someone Dies*—**A Valuable Legal Resource**
- **Organize Your Paperwork**
- **Assets Minus Liabilities Equals Net Worth**
- **Plan Your Final Ceremony**

I have to admit the intensity of my interest in this chapter is low. I hate paperwork. So many decisions. I don't feel secure in knowing what I'm doing legally. I get bored with filing. I wish I had an assistant who thinks like I do so I could delegate it all—perhaps this is why people hire lawyers to do the work for them, an expensive cop out. But I'm the only one who can make most of the decisions. And as much as I dislike doing it, I want my records done my way. Each situation is unique and personal. And none of it will go away. So what to do?

Buy a book! Buy a book that covers all the legal details in clear, simple, non-technical language. A readable book—not in legalese you have to translate. Have you ever seen a book written by a lawyer in plain English? Well, I found one, probably because it was written by a journalist working with the lawyer.

Buy *When Someone Dies: The Practical Guide to the Logistics of Death*, by Scott Taylor Smith with Michael Castleman.[1] It's 150 pages of useful information followed by an appendix of legal forms you can revise to fit your own state. Scott Smith, the lawyer worked with journalist Castelman to help write it after Smith's mother's death. He had discovered how much detail and time was involved in handling her affairs. So it's personal and practical. It begins with a quick reference guide to help you find what you need. Each chapter begins with a checklist of what will be covered. It's loaded with useful information and has an excellent index. Get a copy. It will make your job much easier.

ORGANIZE YOUR PAPERWORK

Now we're back to where you and I begin to update and organize paperwork. I go to the file cabinet where I keep all my documents. I have one drawer that holds all my end-of-life legal papers. I keep a separate file for each document, with a record of who got a copy when, plus any revisions and who got those. I send copies of some documents to many people, some to only a few. But I need to know when and to whom I sent each one so they can get revisions. Now I'm going to offer you my most creative contribution to this chapter: the Routing Record I use for each of my end-of life documents. I've been developing this low-tech device for a few years now and know it works. It replaces memory.

After the title of the document are ticklers for reviewing it at various times: once a year after filing your tax return (this is a must), and after each of the 5 Ds—Decade, Death, Divorce, Diagnosis and Decline. Any of the 5 Ds should cause you to consider necessary changes. It is likely you have made changes in the Decade just passed. A Death may have occurred that triggers a revision. Or perhaps a Divorce has occurred—yours or someone

ROUTING RECORD				
Document Title:				
Review: April 15 and 5Ds: Death, Decade, Decline, Diagnosis, Divorce				
Sent to:	Original Date	Rev. 1 Date	Rev. 2 Date	Rev. 3 Date
Personal Files				

else's—that requires making changes to your documents. Perhaps your physical condition is changing and you've received a new Diagnosis that could change your timeline. You may have begun experiencing a Decline that prompts you to check with your doctor and to review some of your documents. Add a sixth D: Do Not Delay. As soon as you become conscious that you've gotten behind, drop everything and get current again.

This Routing Record is a simple, flexible device that can make your life much simpler. You need to know when and to whom you gave each document. Top-down, I list those names first, with the date I gave it to them. Then I start from the bottom up, under Personal Files, I list the master copy, my original signed copy, and any extras on hand—all of the same date.

I have the first Durable Power of Attorney for Health Care and Health Care Directive that I got when I first moved to Washington. I went to a lawyer, not knowing what I needed, and got everything anyone could ever legally ask for. That wasn't what I wanted—but I didn't know that yet. I wanted the kind of documents you found in Chapters 1 and 2 that are written according to my values and decisions.

After clarifying what I wanted, I had the first document revised and put the original Routing Record on the revision, including to whom I sent it, on what date. In the revision column of the Routing Record, I record the date I sent it to each care giver. At the bottom, under Personal Files, I note the dates I sent it to my personal trustees. The nitty-gritty details we're taking care of here can make a huge difference when you need them. That's the reason I give them such detailed attention. Do it once, maintain it, and you're set.

By the way, the hospital you are most likely to use should have your key documents on file: your Durable Power of Attorney for Health Care (DPOA-HC), your Health Care Directive, and your POLST (or your state's equivalent). This covers you in any emergency—no one has to hunt for your papers or wonder if they're in a safe deposit box, with the bank being closed on the weekend you need them. I suggest you get them witnessed and notarized to cover all risks, even if your state doesn't require it. You may want to take these documents with you when you travel. Not all states have the same requirements. Play it safe.

I can't recall ever taking time out to reorganize my files. I just add to them, buy another cabinet, do whatever takes the least time. The day of reckoning will come—for me, for you and for our heirs. So let's get to work and figure out what documents should be filed together and be easy to find.

The first project is to find and organize the files you already have. What's missing? One starting place is to have a Master List of all the files you need to end your life as you wish and close your personal and business affairs. Put all these in the same file cabinet, with the Master List in front. Here is an example of a list, but how you organize yours will depend on how you think. You will find more options in *When Someone Dies.*

End-of-Life Documents

- Durable Power of Attorney–Health Care, with Consent to Serve
- Durable Power of Attorney–Property/Finances (optional)
- Organ Donation, Autopsy, other final disposition instructions
- Physician Orders for Life Sustaining Treatments (POLST or equivalent)

Funeral Instructions

- Church or a Cremation Society to make cremation arrangements
- DIY–Do It Yourself Services, green cemeteries (eco-friendly)
- Donations–Suggestions to friends of where to donate to chosen organizations
- Durable Power of Attorney–Funeral (optional)
- Memorial Society or Mortuary (burial arrangements)
- Military Options–Special provisions available for military service
- Other Choices–Obituary, flowers, music, leaflets, other

Will or Trust

- This document specifies how you want your property and personal goods distributed after your death, and may provide special handling for certain heirs
- State laws vary. Use a lawyer in your state

<u>Medical Records</u> (list with contact information)

- Primary Care Physician
- Specialists (a separate file for each)

<u>Legal Resources</u>

- Conservator/Guardian (if applicable)
- Elderlaw attorney and other specialties as needed

<u>Investment Counselors</u>

List firm name, representative, phone or email address, account numbers and location of documents

<u>Insurance: Policy #, Phone #, Due Date, Amount, Beneficiary for Each</u>

- Automobile
- Accidental Death
- Health Insurance
- Home Insurance
- Home Security System
- Life Insurance
- Long Term Health Care
- Medicare
- Rental (per rental agreement)
- Social Security
- Other

WHAT INFORMATION DO YOU NEED TO DETERMINE YOUR NET WORTH?

More than likely someone—your Executor or Personal Representative—is going to have to establish your Net Worth. This would be your Assets minus your Liabilities. So your Master List must include the financial information and resources needed to close your estate along with where they're located and how they can be accessed. See the Master List below, choose those items that apply to you.

<u>Bank Accounts</u> (and how to access—passwords or other)

    Bank–Checking: receives Social Security and any other direct deposit income

    Bank–Business, Family, Pay-on-Death Account

    Bank–Savings Accounts

<u>Investment and Securities Accounts</u>

<u>Credit Card Balances</u>

<u>Student Loan Balances</u>

<u>Home Loans (and Reverse Mortgages)</u>

    Current Balance–Lender–Terms

<u>Other Real Estate</u>

    Current Balance–Lender–Terms

<u>Other Debts</u>

    Current Balance–Lender–Terms

<u>Tax Liabilities</u>

    Internal Revenue Service

    Property–Other

You've listed the resources on hand to take care of the end of your life and the business of your life. Now how about the rest of your life, the people and activities that make your life work: your most trusted and helpful friends and their contact numbers; organizations; your address book with all your family members' contacts; subscriptions; passwords, and so on. That list will grow as you think of more items to add to it. Making reference to their location on your computer may be sufficient.

Start by listing your basic team, so your Executor knows whom to contact for key services. These are your primary resources, and they will become your executor's resources. Put this list up front with the Master List:

Basic Team

- Lawyer or elderlaw attorney
- Primary care physician, other health care specialists
- Accountant or bookkeeper
- Investment counselor and any other key professionals you use
- Durable Power of Attorney for Health Care
- Durable Power of Attorney for Finances/Property
- Friends who were available when needed

Your lists are brilliant, your files will look great, and your important documents will be resplendent with their Routing Records attached. Congratulations! And now we're ready to make the final plans for your earthly remains and how to say goodbye from beyond. You may need to organize that too.

PLAN YOUR FINAL CEREMONY

Next is the "party" planning—the final funeral or memorial arrangements for family and friends. Many people are guided by their religion or family customs when they plan a final ceremony. Whether or not that's your choice, cost will likely be a defining factor. The average cost of a full-service funeral and burial is currently between $6 to $8,000, many are over $12,000. Cremation costs about one-third to one-fourth of traditional burial costs. Green burial offers other options.

What is a green cemetery or a green burial? These new practices use eco-friendly principles to be as gentle with the earth as possible. Consider the following facts gathered by Mark Harris, author of *Grave Matters: A Journey Through the Modern Funeral Industry to a Natural Way of Burial.* He says that a typical 10-acre swatch of cemetery ground contains enough coffin wood to construct 40 houses; nearly 1,000 tons of casket steel; 20,000 tons of vault concrete; and enough toxic embalming fluid to fill a backyard swimming pool.[2]

Roy Jacobson spelled it out in the *South Whidbey Record* a few years ago. To get around such old practices, green burial includes placing unembalmed bodies in eco-friendly containers, such as "shrouds, or biodegradable coffins made of cardboard, biodegradable plastic, fair-trade-certified bamboo, pine wood, recycled paper, form-aldehyde-free plywood or hand-woven willow or wicker."[3] Some of these costs can bring total costs up to traditional burial totals.

Use of cremation is rapidly rising compared to traditional burial customs. About 2.5 million people die each year in the United States. In 2011, according to NBC News, 42 percent were cremated, double what it was 15 years ago. The rate varies considerably by state. Washington was 70 percent, Nevada 74 percent, but Mississippi was lowest at 15.7 percent. Religious beliefs affect these decisions—the higher the denomination membership, the lower the cremations in that state. Each denomination has its own beliefs and traditions. For example, the Catholic Church has moved from disallowing cremation to reluctantly accepting it in 1963. Ancient traditions in the Jewish faith say NO, as do Muslims. Buddhists have no objection to cremation, and Hindus mandate it as one of their 16 life rituals.

The Federal Trade Commission instituted the Funeral Rule in 1984, amending it in 1994. It requires funeral providers to give complete written information on costs of services offered to grieving families.

Summarized, here are the consumer protections the Funeral Rule provides:

- You have the right to choose the funeral goods and services you want, with some exceptions.
- The funeral provider must give you a General Price List (GPL) that states your right to choose what you want in writing.
- If state or local law requires you to buy any particular goods or service, the funeral provider must disclose it on the statement it provides, describing the funeral goods and services you have selected, with a reference to the specific law.
- The funeral provider cannot refuse to handle a casket or urn you bought elsewhere—or charge you a fee to do that.

- A funeral provider who offers cremations must make alternative containers available.

- You can't be charged for embalming that your family didn't authorize unless embalming is required by state law.

When it comes time to talk with funeral directors, you may want to read the whole Funeral Rule. It answers many questions. Search "Funeral Rules" online. They also publish, free of charge, *Funerals: A Consumer Guide*, available on the Federal Trade Commission website, *www.ftc.gov*, or through your local Federal Consumers Alliance.

The shift from burial to cremation is largely due to cost savings: it costs about one-third of the cost of burial, no casket nor perpetual cemetery care is needed, and it uses less urban real estate. You can expect to see the trend toward cremation continue, according to Tyler Mathisen in a CNBC report in 2013.[4]

The Funeral Consumers Alliance at *www.funerals.org* is a non-profit volunteer organization that continually monitors funeral legislation and advocates for consumer protection. It is small but quite effective in what it does. FCA helps people form local area associations that offer quality discount memorial services for reduced prices. For example, People's Memorial Association, a nonprofit organization, serves the Seattle area and charges a one-time membership fee of $35. They broker lower costs with local funeral homes and funeral goods providers and inform members of options available to them. For resources in your area contact FCA.

A Funeral Home Price Survey was one of the valuable benefits offered by People's Memorial in 2011. Out of 47 funeral homes in the Seattle area, eight participated in People's Memorial. Prices shown were for the mortuaries' regular rates for direct cremation, direct burial and full funeral service. Funeral homes that participated in People's Memorial offered reduced rates. Between the Funeral Rule and these prices, you had the basic information you needed to figure your own cost range. For example in 2011 People's Memorial prices were: Direct Cremation $699, Direct Burial $1,099, and Full Funeral Service $2,399. Compare those prices with the priciest mortuary in the same area: Direct Cremation $3,944, Direct Burial $3,890, and Full Funeral Service $8,415. (Their new cost survey shows prices for

People's Memorial only, which have remained the same as in 2011. You can call neighborhood mortuaries to get price comparisons.)

Another resource is *www.funeralethics.org/rights* which shows details of consumer rights by state, including limits on the $225.00 Social Security survivor benefit. It may tell you more than you want to know, but if you have to be your own expert, it could be helpful.

As you can see, the details can be endless. Just let me mention a few more useful resources.

- Get FCA's folder that lists educational brochures they publish on key questions. They also include miscellaneous books they handle and other commercial items.

- If you travel, you'll want their Directory of U.S. member funeral homes. My 2006 directory shows 120 locations in 39 states. I'm sure there are more by now. They also have a pamphlet called *"Death Away From Home"* which includes foreign travel. You may want to consider travel insurance when flying.

- A short version of the first part of this chapter is in an excellent booklet called, *"Before I Go, You Should Know"* which shows "My Funeral and Final Plans," complimented by several wonderfully gloomy Edward Gorey cartoons.

- Should you prepay your funeral? It is generally discouraged. You or the funeral provider may move and not notify each other, you may not get all your money back if you cancel, you may forget that you've taken care of that and fail to notify your Personal Representative. Too much to remember at a time of loss and grief. See further information in the FTC booklet, *"Funerals: A Consumer Guide,"* pages 4–5.

- In addition to organ donation requests, there are several medical devices that can be recycled: pacemakers, glasses, hearing aids, insulin pumps, walkers, high-rise toilet seats, shower stools. And don't forget your hair—they make wigs out of it. Senior Centers usually know where to donate.

Budget according to your means. Don't let a funeral home sell you more than you want. With them, it's a business transaction; to you, it's usually a one-time remembrance. Consider cremation or green burial. Not only are these ways more economical, they are more respectful of our planet. But if you choose a more expensive route for your own good reasons, you have considered your options. Your decisions are right for you.

It's not uncommon for people to write their obituaries in writing classes. It's a good way to really think about all the items you want to include, and the tone you want to set. I've seen three kinds of obits:

- The standard reportage of when and how they died, significant activities of the deceased, first generation of remaining relatives, and if "No Flowers" are requested, where to donate. Standard reportage is run-of-the-mill, often written by the mortuary. Leaves you unemotionally informed. End of message.

- The second kind of obit is a warm memory-book account of the wonderful things the person did in their lifetime, including special family events. Can be heartwarming, like a last visit down memory lane with the loved one. Leaves you with warm memories and perhaps a few tears. Often written by friends or family, but preferably written by *you*. There is so much *you* can share that no one else would know about. It's your opportunity to say good-bye the way you want to be remembered.

- The third kind of obit is the maverick report that speaks the truth, the whole truth, but only some of it. This one is rare. I've seen only one like it. It speaks the unvarnished truth. Here's how it starts: "John Paul Jones (not his real name), a brilliant, creative artist and fine woodworker with a gentle loving soul, took his life after courageous battles with shame, depression and alcoholism." This was followed by family details, particularly mentioning his beloved granddaughter. Guests were asked to bring remembrances and a written note for her.

Another preparation you might want to consider is building your own pine box. This is a greater country activity than in the city, but here's one man's experience with it, a thoracic surgeon. The story is called, "Ashes to Ashes, but First a Nice Pine Box," by Jeffrey M. Piehler in the *New York Times*.[5] Not only did he and a woodworker build the pine box, they built a memorable friendship.

Few books are written about end-of life practicalities, but more are coming, thanks to the large Boomer audience. A new bookstore category needs to be created for this literature. I suggest "Obit Lit." and I'd put this book first. If you can tolerate macabre humor, the second book I'd put on that shelf would be *I Died Laughing: Funeral Education with a Light Touch* by Lisa Carlson.[6] It includes much good information and a great many humorous quotes and cartoons. She has long been associated with Funeral Consumers Alliance.

PLAN YOUR FINAL SERVICE

Now for the fun part: you can plan your final service. We each have our own experiences that shape how we want our final moments handled by those who remain behind. Here's my story:

MY GOING-OUT PARTY

When we buried Father in 1995, the cost was $6,300. Now the average funeral can run from $6,000 to $10,000 and up. Why should I give the graveyard shift that kind of money (and it'll be more by the time I conk) when instead, I could invite my immediate family to an all-expense-paid going-out party?

Truth is, I'm getting older. I'm unhappy about paying for long term health care insurance to buy services I don't want to need, ever. No one will be on hand to take care of me, like I did for Father, to give me the choice of dying quietly at home. I think I'm facing the prospect of my own death, essentially alone. This party idea gives me a lift.

When Father, at 96, was failing, my brothers, Art and Roger, and I worked out the details of his funeral. Father had said he wanted to be buried alongside Mother in the family plot where she'd been waiting for him for thirty years. The cemetery folks wanted to know, "Does he want to be buried on her right or left side?" Art was assigned the job of going across the street to get the answer from Father.

"How can we be doing this," I said to Roger, *"burying him while he's still alive?"* Roger shrugged helplessly. *"What do you do when they won't tell you what they want?"* I made up my mind never to put my kids in such a predicament. In that moment my going-out party was born.

Art returned, victorious. *"He wants the right side."* I asked why. *"It's how they slept,"* he said. That was more than Art was willing to handle. *"This is why I want to be cremated,"* he said under his breath. *"Get it done and over with."* Roger heartily agreed. Just like that, we joined the more than 45% of the U. S. population who have opted for the fire.

Cremation gives flexibility—and economy—in planning my going-out party. As soon as I'm gone my funeral society's contractor will do her job and deliver the final three or four quarts of ashes to my executor-son who will pay the balance due. Until scatter-day I want my ashes to rest in something classy, perhaps an elegant engraved pewter pot that, emptied, could be passed on like the family silver.

The greatest gift Father gave our family was Westwoods, our 36-acre bit of heaven on Orcas Island, one of the San Juan Islands in the Pacific Northwest. My going-out party will take place there. For almost forty-five years it's been the summer center for family and friends. Our pebbly beach has a huge driftwood tree root that we tied to the shore, the sunsets making you one with the universe. What better place for this last reunion? Well, not exactly a reunion—I won't be there in person—perhaps more of a communion.

The date for this party is, of course, still unknown. Whenever I flicker out, whatever anyone wants to do to mark my heaven-scheduled passing is fine by me. But this party is the main event for those closest to me, and their schedules will decide the time, not mine. It may take a while before they can synchronize a trip to Orcas Island.

I can wait.

My party plan is simple. By the time everyone coordinates their flights *to Sea-Tac airport from Atlanta, Boston, Jackson, Wyoming and Corte Madera, California, probably six to ten people will be coming. They'll arrive from the mainland, either by plane at the tiny Eastsound airport or by ferry at the thumpy Orcas landing where someone will pick them up in our old red Ford Ranger truck. They'll shed their city armor as each mile takes them deeper into the quieting, sun-dappled woods. Perhaps they'll see deer. Finally, they'll pull up to our white-trimmed forest-green cabin, grab their luggage and clomp onto the deck, take in the sparkling view across the waters, and settle into the knotty pine living room with the welcoming corner brick fireplace. Home again.*

I have three requests for my last event. The first is that everyone makes time to speak together of their memories—tough as well as tender stories that have shaped us as a family.

The second is that someone scatter my ashes off the end of our landmark dock. Some background music would be nice, perhaps Gershwin's "Rhapsody in Blue." I can visualize someone swinging a wide swath of ash-flow way out over the water, freeing my spirit to the Great Spirit. If someone were to hand-inscribe a small memorial plaque and nail it to the dock, I'd like that.

My very last request is that my guests start planning their going-out parties in whatever way they choose. I've let it be known what I'd like. Now, it's theirs to decide.

CHAPTER SEVEN

GET ON WITH LIVING

*True power comes from aligning what you deeply value
with your words and actions in the world.*
—David Weinstock

Congratulations! Now that you have finished the work in the first six chapters, you've done all you can to take care of yourself as the end of your life nears. This assumes that you continue contact with your Agent, and that you watch for health care provisions you may want to make in your Health Care Directive. Remember, after I learned more about it, I realized I wanted to add surgery to my DO NOT want list. If I'm not terminal, I can always change my mind. If I am terminal, NO works fine for me—or my Agent will know what else to do.

One key purpose of making all these decisions early is to be informed of what's possible, and have time to decide what you want for yourself at your end of life. Like most of us, you may not have enough information to decide some things. You may want to read up on new developments, or talk with your doctor about possible consequences.

Medicare plays a huge role for the older generation and change happens slowly. But now you can consult with your doctor and Medicare will pay her/him for time spent on end-of-life counseling. They finally have decided that: "We think these discussions are an important part of patient- family-centered care." [1]

They seem to give their full blessing to this function. "...their length can vary based on patients' needs... Sometimes they're short conversations—the person has thought about it. Sometimes, they're a much longer conversation. Sometimes, they're a series of conversations."[2]

Filling out forms only is of limited value. The ongoing conversation and continuing relationship with your Agent and physician is what works best. Dr. Diane Meier, Director of Center to Advance Palliative Care, said, "I think it's great news that Medicare... is now formally recognizing that advance planning is worthy of its attention and reimbursement, and that, in fact, is a way to restore power and control to patients."[3] That is the whole purpose of this book—to restore power and control to patients.

Of course, there are varying views on how this provision could be misused, but Dr. Joseph Hinterberger in rural upstate New York, who has been doing free end-of-life discussions, has this view: "I think what it will mostly do is decrease confusion at the end of life," he said. "It will potentially decrease unnecessary use of resources because it will be very clear what the patient did and did not want. And it should also make it easier for physicians and other caregivers to make decisions because they can say, 'We all know what Mildred's wishes were. We shall not tread upon them.'" It makes me feel good to know that Medicare finally agrees with me. Focus is now on the patient's decisions.[4]

And that is the whole point of this book—for each of us to affirm that the end of our lives will come, that we will learn to accept that fact and take responsibility by making decisions only we can make. Others may try to do it for us so their wishes would prevail, not ours. But it is still your choice, your decision to define how you wish your life to end—to fit the beliefs you hold dear. You can make requests of others, you can choose renderings of music or readings that you love, you can make special requests that give you deep satisfaction. These are acts of freedom—and acceptance.

So take charge. Let your end come the way you choose. It's a gift of life.

ACKNOWLEDGMENTS

It all began with my hairdresser, Mary Lint, who found the topic gripping. She never lost interest in it, and swore she'd sell books out of her salon—so hurry up and finish it, she'd say. I'd read it to her, chapter by chapter, as it slowly progressed.

On September 23, 2009, the local newspaper published my article on the POLST (Physician Orders for Life Sustaining Treatments). I had sought advance approval from local EMT staff headed by Paul Zaveruha, MD, managed by Roger Meyer, with Robert May in public relations. They have been most supportive, as was Geri Forbes, new CEO in 2016, of the local hospital—being renamed WhidbeyHealth.

My research led to being unexpectedly appointed to Washington's POLST Task Force, sponsored by Washington's End of Life Coalition. There I met several forward thinkers: Bruce C. Smith, MD, Richard L. Sayre, JD, and Sharmon Figenshaw, ARNP, ACHPN, all experts on thinking through how the POLST could best be adapted in the differing health care facilities responsible for using it. Amy Vandenbroucke, JD, Executive Director, National POLST Paradigm, added to this rich input. Through writing this book, I found the excellent work of Bernard "Bud" Hammes, medical ethicist and developer of Wisconsin's Respecting Choices, and Honoring Choices offered in other states and Australia. The goal is to inspire and support community-based conversations among adults of all ages about end-of-life care planning, and to share these plans with loved ones and health care teams.

When you live in a small, well-knit community for several years, networks of friendships evolve through participating in our many activities and interests. Our Whidbey community has a never-ending supply of creative energy, so one can be busy as long as your health holds up. Even with serious health issues in my late 80's, I managed to finish this book. My thanks to my doctors, Peter Sutcliffe, MD, Tom Harris, OD, and especially Cathy Robinson, PA-C. Add other kinds of freely offered support from Peter and Anna Marie Morton, Ed and Chris Halloran, Gary and Rubye Vallat, Sam Glass and Donna Vanderheiden, David and Mavis Cauffman, John and Miriam Raabe, David and Cynthia Trowbridge, Sally Elder and Kent Vandervelde, Shirley Owen, Michael Moch, and Karl Harris.

Some of these friends participate in a one-of-a-kind group called Philodox, founded by curmudgeon Malcolm Ferrier, which means "lovers of ideas, especially our own." A varying group of about eight men and four women meet every Monday morning, even on holidays, for two hours of social, humorous, educational, thoughtful conversation on a topic suggested during the week, or on whatever else is on our minds.

We even have a resident poet. It's addictive, necessary, fun and stimulating. Where else would I learn about 3-D printing—with actual samples? It gives a crisp start to the week. I love this group.

My other community resources include contacts with our artists, musical people and those interested in end-of-life concerns. Add Claudia and Tom Walker, Sharon Spencer, Peggy Rudolph, Sue Wright, Ann Cutcher, MD, Nikki Coyote, Louise Fiori, Diane Ahuna, Solveig Lee, Corrine Bayley, Cynthia Trenshaw, Gerry Simpson, Judy Simpson, Katy Shaner, Stephanie Neis and Sally Salazar. Several participate in local groups such as the Saratoga Symphony, Rural Characters, Whidbey Threshold Singers, Enso House, and Whidbey Island Center for the Arts. Even my life-long friend in Seattle, Donna Stringer, and her husband Andy, frequently schedule together-time.

My most supportive first generation family, who live far from Whidbey, includes son David Kuettel, son Steven Kuettel and grandson Ben, nephew Robert Westmont, plus step-daughter Dolly Prince. The only author in my family is cousin Jeff Westmont, *Countdown to Jihad*. Adopted family: I'm Gramma to Ani Bulbulian, and close friend to her mother, Rachel. I also have the rare privilege of being Gramma to their six cats: Anoush, Coco, Topaz, Hagop, Daisy and Pippi. Ani's favorite, Topaz, has thick white fur accented by one blue—and one topaz—eye.

A remarkable writing community has grown up here, aided by our local Whidbey Island Writers Association. Andrea Hurst, agent and developmental editor, holds supportive weekly group writing sessions at the end of the Coupeville pier. Friends who have published books since I came to Whidbey are: Mary Knight, *Saving Wonder;* Garr Kuhl, *Snagged: The Door to ZEE, Captured: A Retro Ransford Adventure,* and *Guadalajara Burn: A Skip Reid Adventure Thriller* (Mary, Garr and I were a weekly writing group for about three years); Catherine W. Scherer, *The Internationalists: Masters of the Global Game;* Miriam Sonn Raabe, *Bite into the Day;* Allen Ament, *Learning to Float;* Dorothy Read, *End the Silence;* Ann Linnea, *Keepers of the Trees;* and Christina Baldwin, *The Seven Whispers, Storycatcher: Making Sense of Our Lives through the Power and Practice of Story, Life's Companion: Journal*

Writing as a Spiritual Practice (revised, reissued), *The Circle Way*. Finally, Connie Dawson, *Life Beyond Shame: Rewriting the Rules.* And I must mention another friend, Barbara Joy Laffey, who put her book on hold while she completed her PhD dissertation.

Creative professionals who contributed to the publishing of this book are internal designer Susan Prescott, editor Dorothy Read, marketing consultants Alice Acheson and Peter Morton, and technical consultants Shelly Loewen and Steve Sloan. I am also indebted to lawyer Scott Taylor Smith with Michael Castleman. Chapter Six, with Scott's permission, is built around his helpful book, *When Someone Dies: The Practical Guide to the Logistics of Death.*[1]

The energy is here. Little did I realize what a community project this book could become. My heartfelt appreciation to all these friends. I love you all (and any others hanging out in the memory-shadows). Thank you.

HISTORIC CHANGES 1975–2005

In those thirty years—between 1975 and 2005—a cluster of entwined changes were occurring that changed how we die, and therefore, how we live. The roots of some of these changes began during the prior decade—and I expect clusters of changes to continue as the Boomers start facing their mortality. As a group, they are likely to take a more active stance toward creating better health futures.

Here are some highlights of events unfolding during that time.

- Medical technology was rapidly advancing. Take ventilators. From iron lungs, to the Salk vaccine which stopped polio, to bulky **respirators** and ventilators, to full ICU units. **Cases of persistent vegetative state (PVS)** began to appear, starting with Quinlan. In cardiology, **CPR** started hearts beating and the **defibrillator** made racing, out-of-control hearts suddenly beat normally. **Feeding tubes** were, at first, strung through nose-to-stomach, then advanced to tracheotomies—a hole in the throat—to more permanent fixtures implanted for direct delivery to the stomach, with auxiliary in-and-out tubes. Innovation was accelerating and contagious.

- The first successful **heart transplant** in the U.S. occurred in 1968, the same year that the Uniform Anatomical Gift Act was passed, and created the **"Donor Card"** and allowed families to consent to or refuse donation. This opened a whole new field of other organs to transplant, including the pancreas, heart and lung as a unit, corneas, heart valves, skin, bone, bone marrow, partial livers, intestines, blood vessels, tendons and ligaments—a whole new world. At the beginning, the biggest problem was the rejection of the new organ by the old immune system. In 1983, the FDA approved **cyclosporine,** which reduced the rejection problem, and sparked a huge increase in transplants. But you couldn't even think of selling your organs—or anyone else's—after 1984 when the **National Organ Transplant** Act prohibited that thought. It set up a national transplant network, **United Network for Organ Sharing (UNOS),** to procure and distribute organs on a fair basis. This was tricky, since the demand far exceeded the supply then, and still does today. International implications were not yet recognized.

- A thoughtful **Patient's Bill of Rights** was developed by the American Hospital Association in 1973, revised in 1992, that clearly set up collaborative decision-making with the patient, the doctor, the hospital and staff. It notes that all of their activities must be done with "an overriding concern for the values and dignity of patients."

- The **Uniform Brain Death Act** was passed in 1978, which expanded for the first time the traditional definition of death. "Brain death" is death, but so is no heartbeat/no breathing. So "what to do with two definitions of death" was the issue of the day.

- Two technological advances—the respirator and transplantation—led to the need for a **redefinition of death,** a task completed by a Presidential Commission in 1981. Before then, the absence of a heartbeat and breathing indicated death. Quoting the report, the importance of a beating heart in a living person is challenged when, after a heart transplant, "a 'dead' person's heart can beat in the chest of a 'living' person whose own heart has not merely stopped but has been removed from his or her body." They also dealt with the effects of mechanical respirators that "enabled physicians to reverse the failure of respiration and circulation in many victims of … cardiac arrest… "but which could cause irreversible damage to the brain, including the brain stem. Proof of that much damage "provides a highly reliable means of declaring death…"

- *Deciding to Forego Life-Sustaining Treatment,* a 1983 government report, delved into ethical, medical and legal questions. It reconsidered conclusions in the 1981 report, *Defining Death,* and included conclusions arrived at in the 2008 report, *Controversies in the Determination of Death.*

- But some folks were focused on keeping people alive. In 1967 the **emergency 911 system** was being devised, and gradually grew so that by 1987, over 50% of the U.S. population had access, with most all of us having it by 2000.

- The first training of **Emergency Medical Technician (EMT)** staffs began in 1969, **paramedics** joined the system, and they all merged into **the emergency 911** system as it grew nationally.

- **CPR, cardiopulmonary resuscitation,** was presented to the National Academy of Sciences in 1966, resulting in doctors and other health providers learning how to do it, and to see if laypersons could also learn it.

- The **right to privacy** arose as a result of the invention of **"the Pill,"** the first oral contraceptive, a crime under Connecticut law that wound up in the Supreme Court, which ruled in 1965 that the state could not rule in this private area.

- Eight years later, in 1973, that principle was applied to *Roe v. Wade,* which aroused the **battle between pro-choice and pro-life movements,** still alive and well today.

- Natural Death Acts, or "Right-to-die" laws came out of Quinlan in 1976, linked to common law concepts of **informed consent** and **personal autonomy.** The principle was then formulated that:

  > "Every human being of adult years and sound mind has a right
  > to determine what shall be done with his body; and a surgeon
  > who performs an operation without his patient's consent com-
  > mits an assault, for which he is liable in damages."[1]

- **"Substituted judgment"** came from *Quinlan.* How could a person in a coma or persistent vegetative state refuse treatment? Her incapacity shouldn't deprive her of her rights. So the judges allowed those who knew her when she was healthy, and knew her values or wishes, to substitute their judgment for hers. They were still struggling with how to **define the PVS diagnosis,** which took until the early 1980s.

- Consider the patient who wants to refuse a medical treatment but isn't able to say so. **Living wills** were invented by Luis Kutner for just that patient. Who was Kutner and why did he care? Between 1930 and 1960, he had become a high-profile human rights attorney. He co-founded Amnesty International plus the World Habeas Corpus project for people unfairly imprisoned around the world. The **power of the person** was what he cared about. Thus, his 1969 law journal article proposed the living will as a way for the patient to specify their wishes for any future health disasters.

- All these connecting issues led to forming the **profession of bioethicists** in the 1980s, which came to a consensus that **artificial nutrition and hydration (ANH)** was a life-sustaining medical treatment that could legally be refused.

- Since proxies were getting more involved in these sticky cases, many states set up an order of "who ranked whom" in **family hierarchies** to make decisions patients could no longer make. So more state laws were passed.

- In 1990 the feds passed the **Patient Self Determination Act,** which required hospitals to ask patients about proxies and living wills to guide their care while hospitalized. It promoted, but did not require **advance directives,** especially for terminal patients.

- Most notable of all the changes was the **huge increase in life expectancy,** which was age 47 in 1900 and age 77 in 2000. It has been touted as "the greatest single achievement in history," which it may well be. But it may also be the greatest headache. We used to die in a couple of weeks, maybe a month. Now we take closer to two years to die of chronic diseases—and that costs money.

- We used to die of old age. Today you can't. Today **you have to die of a disease** from an official list of 113, or the doctor can't complete your death certificate. **Old age is not a disease,** therefore you can't die of it.

- Because of these patterns, a **four-year study of "how we die in America"** was done between 1989 and 1995, with an investigative, then intervention phase. Entitled **SUPPORT,** it was funded mostly by The Robert Wood Johnson Foundation and George Soros. The first phase involved over 9,000 seriously ill patients, about 5,000 of whom died during the study. It laid the groundwork for further educational efforts and more communication on End-of-Life information and decisions.

- Care for the dying—who were now taking so long to die—helped create the addition of **hospice** in 1986 when a Medicare hospice benefit was made permanent by Congress. Terminal patients could get care in their dying process, free of life-sustaining treatments, and were relieved of spending expensive time in ICUs. They could enjoy involving their families in activities leading to a more compassionate dying.

- In 1994, Oregon passed the **first Death with Dignity Act** with a 51 percent vote. It was challenged by the National Right to Life Committee, so Oregon voted again and agreed not to rescind it, and it passed with a 60 percent vote. So it was not until 1997 that "Helen," the first person to use it, died by using legal medication.

  Dr. Ira Byock, widely-known for his end-of-life contributions to SUPPORT and hospice development, comments in *Last Rights: Rescuing the End of Life from the Medical System* by Stephen P. Kiernan, "...medical science is reluctant to admit that for every single patient eventually its methods and disciplines fail....

  "Yet death is something virtually every doctor will confront in his or her career, and 100 percent of the population is at risk of needing effective end-of-life intervention. And death gets 24 hours in medical school...even that estimate is generous."[2]

- The conclusion of the Terri Schiavo case in 2005, legally permitted stopping Life Sustaining Treatments (LST) and Allow Natural Death (AND). Legal permission was given to NOT use a LST. End of life became a legal choice of the patient.

CATHOLIC ISSUES / MERGERWATCH

In Chapter 2, I placed a negative emoji (⊘) next to the Health Care Directive where my decisions differed from Catholic moral teachings. Here we focus on issues of mergers between secular and Catholic facilities. Basically, the same issues are involved.

The Ethical and Religious Directives (ERDs) of the Catholic Church, written by the United States Conference of Catholic Bishops (USCCB), govern how health care is to be administered in health care facilities in the U.S. They cover all aspects of life, from birth to death. I suggest you read or scan all or part of them. Search for ERDs and you'll get the full title. A Catholic facility usually will not follow certain provisions in your Advance Directive if they conflict with "Catholic moral teachings." And they may not give you all the information you should have through the Informed Consent process.

Most of the time Catholic hospitals follow the ERDs. However, there are exceptions. I have in hand a printed folder from a Catholic-based hospital. In their Guide to Patient Rights and Responsibilities, I find a couple of commitments that don't seem to follow the ERDs. It says you have a right: *"To have your personal, cultural and spiritual values and beliefs supported when making a decision about treatment."* And another: *"To have your advance directives or living will honored."* And *"...your wishes such as not receiving life sustaining treatments will be honored."*[1] These specifics, if honored, would conflict with several ERDs, some of which are quoted here.

- #24. "…The institution, however, will not honor an advance directive that is contrary to Catholic teaching. If the advance directive conflicts with Catholic teaching, an explanation should be provided as to why the directive cannot be honored."

- #25. "…Decisions by the designated surrogate should be faithful to Catholic moral principles and to the person's intentions and values, or … the person's best interests."

- #28. "… The free and informed health care decision of the person or the person's surrogate is to be followed so long as it does not contradict Catholic principles."

Then comes the most controversial one about end-of-life concerns:

- #58. "In principle, there is an obligation to provide patients with food and water, including medically assisted nutrition and hydration for those who cannot take food orally. This obligation extends to patients in chronic and presumably irreversible conditions (e.g., the "persistent vegetative state") who can reasonably be expected to live indefinitely if given such care." (Comment: in the newer version of the ERDs, the term "presumption" becomes an "obligation" to provide patients with food and water...)

- #61. And here comes the "double effect" rule about pain: "…Medicines capable of alleviating or suppressing pain may be given to a dying person, even if this therapy may indirectly shorten the person's life so long as the intent is not to hasten death. Patients experiencing suffering that cannot be alleviated should be helped to appreciate the Christian understanding of redemptive suffering." (No other option is offered.)

These are some of the limitations on Informed Consent and freedom of speech that don't apply to non-Catholics, nature-lovers or freethinkers. The First Amendment comes to mind: "Congress shall make no law respecting an establishment of religion, or prohibiting the free exercise thereof; or abridging the freedom of speech…"

Catholic facilities are usually committed to these ERD parameters. That is their choice when they follow the rules of their faith. Non-Catholics, in my opinion, should have the same choice to exercise their beliefs in a facility that serves the general public, and who help pay for the church's non-profit status. Many "non-profits" are highly profitable. In exchange, the church should support the individual choices of the general public. This issue has many aspects that are being monitored by Merger-Watch, an organization that supports patients' rights in these mergers. Here is their statement of those issues.

MERGERWATCH—PROTECT PATIENTS' RIGHTS TO INFORMED CONSENT

The MergerWatch Project is working to protect patient's rights to make treatment decisions based on complete accurate medical advice and the patient's own religious and ethical beliefs, without interference from institutional religious doctrine or individual providers' religious beliefs.

We seek to harness the collective power of a broad-based coalition of consumer groups, health care providers and public policymakers to advocate for the following protections:

- Protecting patient's rights to INFORMED CONSENT made with knowledge of all potential treatment options, (including those prohibited by a health provider due to religious policies).

- Requiring advance DISCLOSURE to patients of any religious-based policies that restrict patients' access to medical information or services at hospitals, health systems and clinics, or in the coverage offered by health insurers.

- Requiring needed services in case of EMERGENCY, or when no alternate provider exists, even if the service conflicts with institutional religious doctrine.

- Requiring alternate REFERRALS to alternate providers, for non-emergency care when institutional policies forbid the provision of needed services.

- Requiring that hospitals and nursing homes honor patients health care proxies and ADVANCE DIRECTIVES or disclose in advance any restrictions on honoring the patient's wishes. When patient's wishes conflict with hospital policy, the hospital or nursing home should be prepared to arrange a transfer to an alternate facility that is located within a reasonable geographic distance and will accept the patient's health insurance coverage.

—from the MergerWatch website; "Working to Protect Patients' Rights", *mergerwatch.squarespace.com/patients-rights*. The MergerWatch Project: Protecting Patients' Rights When Hospitals Merge. An affiliate of Community Catalyst, a national consumer health advocacy organization..

HIPPOCRATIC OATH: MODERN VERSION

I swear to fulfill, to the best of my ability and judgment, this covenant:

I will respect the hard-won scientific gains of those physicians in whose steps I walk, and gladly share such knowledge as is mine with those who are to follow.

I will apply, for the benefit of the sick, all measures [that] are required, avoiding those twin traps of overtreatment and therapeutic nihilism.

I will remember that there is art to medicine as well as science, and that warmth, sympathy, and understanding may outweigh the surgeon's knife for the chemist's drug.

I will not be ashamed to say "I know not," nor will I fail to call in my colleagues when the skills of another are needed for a patient's recovery.

I will respect the privacy of my patients, for their problems are not disclosed to me that the world may know. Most especially must I tread with care in matters of life and death. If it is given me to save a life, all thanks. But it may also be within my power to take a life; this awesome responsibility must be faced with great humbleness and awareness of my own frailty. Above all, I must not play at God.

I will remember that I do not treat a fever chart, a cancerous growth, but a sick human being, whose illness may affect the person's family and economic stability. My responsibility includes these related problems, if I am to care adequately for the sick.

I will prevent disease whenever I can, for the prevention is preferable to cure.

I will remember that I remain a member of society, with special obligations to all my fellow human beings, those sound of mind and body as well as the infirm.

If I do not violate this oath, may I enjoy life and art, respected while I live and remembered with affection thereafter. May I always act so as to preserve the finest traditions of my calling and may I long experience the joy of healing those who seek my help.

—*Written in 1964 by Louis Lasagna, Academic Dean of the School of Medicine at Tufts University, and used in many medical schools today.*[1]

NOTES

Preface

1. Lachs, Mark S., MD, MPH, and Pellemer, Karl A., Ph.D., N Engl J Med 2015; 373:1947–1956, Nov. 12, 2015, DOI: 10.1056/NEJMra1404688.

2. Oliver Sacks, *Gratitude.* New York: Alfred A. Knopf, 2015, front cover flap, p. 20.

Introduction–The Puzzle

1. Revised Code of Washington (RCW): 20–122.

Chapter 1–Durable Power of Attorney for Health Care

1. Nathan Heller, "Why Are So Many Americans Single?" New Yorker (April. 2012).

2. Nancy P. King, *Making Sense of Advance Directives.* (Washington D.C: Springer Publishing, 1996) p. 125.

Chapter 2–Health Care Directive (Living Will)

1. Virginia Morris, *Talking About Death.* (Chapel Hill, NC: Algonquin Books, 2004) p. 43.

2. Generalized from Richard A. Leiter, Ed., *National Survey of State Laws,* 4th Ed. (Farmington Hills, MI: Thomson-Gale, 2003) pp. 489–504.

3. "Catholic moral teachings" *Health Progress* (Jan-Feb. 2010) p. 71. (Quoting U.S. Conference of Catholic Bishops, "Q and A: The New Directive 58: What Does It Mean?")

4. Ibid.

Chapter 3–Unexpected Events You Didn't Plan For

1. Barbara Peters Smith, "Florida Tests End-of-Life Care Document," *Sarasota Herald Tribune* (July 30, 2013).

2. Carol M. Ostrom, "Doctor's Order Better Conveys Dying Wishes," *The Seattle Times* (May 30, 2005).

3. Robert H. Shmerling, MD, Beth Israel Deaconess Medical Center: *InteliHealth* (January 3, 2010).

4. Eisenberg, MS, MD, *Resuscitate! How Your Community Can Improve Survival from Sudden Cardiac Arrest*. (Seattle: University of Washington Press, 2009) pp. 96–97.

5. Amy Vandenbroucke, National POLST Paradigm, private communication, October 21, 2013.

6. Compassion and Support (New York) *www/compassionandsupport.org/index/for_professionals/molst_training_center/cpr.*

7. Kaufman, S. R., *And a Time to Die: How American Hospitals Shape the End of Life* (Chicago: University of Chicago Press, 2005) pp. 273–288.

8. Quoted and excerpted from Alec MacGillis, "The Unwitting Birthplace of the 'Death Panel' Myth," *The Washington Post* (September 4, 2009).

9. Robert Pear, "Obama Institutes End-of-Life Plan That Caused Stir," *New York Times* (December 30, 2010).

10. Kate Pickert, "The Health Care Proposal that Spawned the 'Death Panels' Lie Is Back," *Time U.S.* (July 25, 2013).

11. Deena Prichep,"Death Cafes Breathe Life Into Conversations About Dying," NPR *www.npr.org* (March 8, 2013).

12. Ibid.

13. Ibid.

14. Rebekah Denn, "Let's Have Dinner and Talk about Death," *Seattle Times Online* (August 22, 2013).

15. American College of Surgeons on Advance Directives by Patients, "Do Not Resuscitate" in the operating room, *Bulletin of the American College of Surgeons* (Vol. 99 No. 1, January 2014) pp. 42–43.

16. Ibid.

17. Barbara Starfield, MD, MPH, "Is U.S. Health Really the Best In the World?," *Journal of the American Medical Association* (Vol. 284, No. 4, July 26, 2000) pp. 483–485.

18. Linda T. Kohn, Janet M Corrigan and Molla S. Donaldson, Editors, *To Err Is Human: Building a Safer Health System.* (Institute of Medicine, Washington D.C: National Academy Press, 1999).

19. Atul Gawande, MD, *The Checklist Manifesto: How to Get Things Right.* (New York: Metropolitan Books, 2010).

Chapter 4 Turning Terminal

1. Sidney Wanzer, MD with J. Glenmullen, MD, *To Die Well.* (Philadelphia: Da Capo Press, 2007).

2. Ibid.

3. Ibid.

4. William J. Peace, "Comfort Care as Denial of Personhood," *Hastings Center Report* (Volume 42, Issue 4, July–August 2012) pp. 14–17.

5. Harriet McBride Johnson, *Too Late to Die Young: Nearly True Tales from a Life.* (New York: Henry Holt and Company, 2005).

6. Joanne Lynn and D.M. Adamson, *Living Well at the End of Life: Adapting Health Care to Serious Chronic Illness in Old Age.* (Washington: Rand Health, 2003).

7. Joanne Lynn, *Sick to Death and Not Going to Take It Anymore!* (Berkeley: University of CA Press, 2004) p. 46.

8. Sharon R. Kaufman, Ph.D, "Chapter 8: Hidden Places: The Zone Of Indistinction As A Way Of Life" in *And a Time to Die: How American Hospitals Shape the End of Life* (Chicago and London: University of Chicago Press, 2005).

9. Brain Injury Association, *www.biausa.org/about-brain-injury.htm.*

10. Wanzer, *To Die Well*, pp. 30–31.

11. Ken Murray, MD, "How Doctors Die," *Utne Reader* (May–June, 2012) 68–69.

12. Wanzer, *To Die Well.*

13. Empowering Caregivers *www.care-givers.com.*

14. Timothy Quill and Margaret P. Battin, *Physician-Assisted Dying: the Case for Palliative Care and Patient Choice.* (Baltimore: The Johns Hopkins University Press, 2004).

15. Stanley A. Terman, PhD, MD, *The Best Way To Say Goodbye: A Legal Peaceful Choice at the End of Life.* (Carlsbad, CA: Life Transitions Publications, 2004).

16. Anemona Hartocollis, "Hard Choice for a Comfortable Death: Sedation," *New York Times* (December 27, 2009).

17. Derek Humphry, *Final Exit: The Practicalities of Self-Deliverance and Assisted Suicide for the Dying,* 3rd Edition. (New York: Dell Publications, 2002).

18. Ibid., p. i.

19. Ibid., p i.

Chapter 5–Communicating to Get Your Decisions Followed

1. Peter M. Murray, MD, "The History of Informed Consent," *Iowa Orthopaedic Journal* (No.10, 1990) pp.104–109.

2. Arthur E. Hertzler, *The Horse and Buggy Doctor.* (Lincoln, NE: University of Nebraska Press, 1970).

3. Sherwin B. Nuland, *How We Die: Reflections on Life's Final Chapter.* (New York: Vintage Books, 1993) pp. 252–254.

4. Ibid.

5. Pauline Chen, MD, *Final Exam: A Surgeon's Reflections on Mortality.* (New York: Vintage Books, 2007) pp. 118–119.

6. Ibid., p. 174.

7. Ibid., p. 167.

8. Jerome Groopman, MD, Pamela Hartzband, MD, *Your Medical Mind: How to Decide What is Right for You.* (New York: Penguin Press, 2011) pp. 168–184.

9. Sherwin Nuland, *How We Die,* p. 258.

10. Pauline Chen, *Final Exam,* p. 147.

11. Ibid., p. 148.

12. Ibid., p. 155.

13. Dr. Ed Creagan quoted by Jeff Hansel in "Mayo Clinic specialist discusses divergent end-of-life scenarios," Rochester *Post-Bulletin.com* (September 11, 2012).

14. Dr. Joanne Lynne, quoted by Jonathan Rauch in "How Not to Die," *The Atlantic* (May 2013) p. 67.

15. Jonathan Rauch, "How Not to Die," *The Atlantic* (May, 2013) pp. 64–69.

16. Theodora Wells, *Keeping Your Cool Under Fire: Communicating Non-Defensively.* (New York: McGraw-Hill, 1980).

17. Ibid.

Chapter 6–Managing Your Paperwork

1. Scott Taylor Smith with Michael Castleman, *When Someone Dies: The Practical Guide to the Logistics of Death.* (New York: Scribner, 2013).

2. Mark Harris, *Grave Matters: A Journey Through the Modern Funeral Industry to a Natural Way of Burial.* (New York: Scribner, 2007).

3. Roy Jacobson, "Cemetery opts for an eco-friendly portal of final departure," *South Whidbey Record* (March 10, 2010) p. 6.

4. Tyler Mathisen, "The Hot Trend in the Funeral Business? Cremation, Of Course," CNBC (Jan. 22, 2013).

5. Jeffrey M. Piehler, "Ashes to Ashes, but First a Nice Pine Box." *New York Times,* (Feb. 1, 2014).

6. Lisa Carlson, *I Died Laughing; Funeral Education with a Light Touch.* (Upper Access, 2001).

Chapter 7–Get On With Living

1. Bellock, Pam, *Medicare Plans to Pay Doctors for Counseling on End of Life, New York Times,* July 8, 2015).

2. Ibid.

3. Ibid.

4. Ibid.

Acknowledgments

1. Scribner, New York, 2013.

Appendix 1: Historic Changes 1975-2005

1. Colby, William H. *Unplugged: Reclaiming Our Right to Die in America..* (New York: American Management Association, 2006) pp. 83–84.

2. Kiernan, Stephen P. *Last Rights: Rescuing the End of Life from the Medical System.* (New York: St. Martin's Press, 2006) p. 87.

Appendix 2: Catholic Issues / MergerWatch

1. Providence Regional Medical Center *Helpful Information for Patients and Families,* #39403 (Everett, Washington: June 19, 2012) p. 13–14.

Appendix 3: Hippocratic Oath—Modern Version

1. Tyson, Peter. *The Hippocratic Oath Today.* NOVA, *www.pbs.org/wgbh/nova/body/hippocratic-oath-today.html,* posted March 27, 2001.

GLOSSARY

ACP: Advance Care Planning The process of learning about and deciding what kind of care you do and don't want as you age—an ongoing educational process. Decisions may change as you age.

Acute Condition (compared to **Chronic Condition**) Acute Condition is serious but fixable—you're expected to recover. **Chronic Condition** is not fixable, just temporarily relieved.

ADs: Advance Directives A record of decisions made during ACP which usually include your Durable Power of Attorney for Health Care and your Health Care Directive (Living Will). They also can include a General or Financial Power of Attorney, a Values Statement, a POLST, depending on state definitions.

ADLs: Activities of Daily Living and **IADLs: Instrumental ADLs** The ability to take certain actions helps determine an aging person's competence to handle their own affairs. ADLs are: dressing, bathing, toileting, eating, walking, transferring between bed/chair. IADLs are: grocery shopping and meal preparation, driving, housework, managing money, managing medication, using telephone and mail.

Agent Legally appointed representative named in your Durable Power of Attorney for Health Care (DPOA-HC). **Attorney-in-Fact** is a common legal term for the same thing, and **Proxy** is also often used. **Agent** is used in this book.

AND: Allow Natural Death Same as **DNR: Do Not Resuscitate.**

ANH: Artificial Nutrition and Hydration A Life Sustaining Treatment. See Ch. 2.

Antibiotics An LST. See Ch. 2.

Assisted Dying (also called Assisted Suicide.) See **Death with Dignity.**

Bioethics Commonly accepted principles of health care ethics that include 1) autonomy, 2) nonmalficence (do no harm), 3) beneficence (do good) and 4) justice.

Blood Transfusion An LST. See Ch. 2.

Chemotherapy An LST. See Ch. 2.

Chronic Condition (cf. **Acute Condition**) A condition that will not get better.

Comfort Care Designed to provide comfort and dignity beyond acute care. Includes pain relief, pain medication, food and water but usually not artificial nutrition and hydration.

CPR: Cardiopulmonary Resuscitation An LST. See Ch. 2.

CPT Codes: Current Procedural Terminology A 5-digit numbering system for pricing medical procedures, surgeries, diagnostics and supplies the patient receives. Copyrighted by AMA, updated yearly, available for a fee.

Critical Care See **ICU: Intensive Care Unit**.

Death An individual is dead who has sustained *either* (1) irreversible cessation of circulatory and respiratory functions, *or* (2) irreversible cessation of all functions of the entire brain, including the brain stem.

Death with Dignity A state law that says if you are terminal, i.e. medically expected to die in 6 months or less, with medical help you can go through a legal process to get a prescription that you must self-administer, that will end your life in a short time. Only CA, OR, NM, VT and WA allow it as we go to press. In MT, a 5-year-old Baxter ruling authorizing medical aid in dying continues to be challenged, but survives.

Dialysis An LST. See Ch. 2.

DNR: Do Not Resuscitate Same as **AND: Allow Natural Death.**

Double Effect Ethical principle that justifies medical treatment that relieves suffering, even when death might be an unintended consequence.

DPOA vs. POA (Durable compared to non-durable Power of Attorney) When you bestow a *durable* POA on a person, they cannot act on it as long as you are able. But when you are unable to act, *then* they can act for you. If you regain some ability to think and decide, their DPOA ceases. However, when you bestow a *non-durable* POA, such as on a bank account, it operates in just the reverse. As long as you can write checks, your POA can also. But when you get dysfunctional or die, the non-durable POA also dies. It's useful for healthy absences, but not for end-of-life situations. (See diagram, Ch. 3)

Effective Immediately Many states have some procedure, usually written certification by two doctors, to decide if you are "decisionally incapacitated"—not able to make decisions. You can bypass this hurdle by making your document Effective Immediately.

Elderlaw Attorneys A recent specialty of the law requiring knowledge of needs of older persons: long term care planning, guardianship, retirement, Social Security, Medicare/Medicaid, special services for this population.

EMS: Emergency Medical Services Starting in 1971 when the national highway system was completed. 9-1-1 has operated in all states for over 40 years.

ERDs: Ethical and Religious Directives Directives of the Catholic Church about health care, especially at the beginning and ending of life, that require observance of Catholic moral teachings in Catholic facilities.

HCD: Health Care Directive (same as **Living Will**) See Ch. 2.

HIPAA: Health Insurance Portability and Accountability Act of 1996 For its terms, see Ch. 1, in my personal DPOA-HC document, under HIPAA Disclosure Authorization.

Hospice Illness has progressed to where curative treatment is no longer desired nor beneficial. Hospice supports patients and families while focusing on relieving symptoms and offering relief from pain, nausea, insomnia, constipation. Also see **Palliative Care.**

ICU: Intensive Care Unit A hospital unit that delivers critical care and close monitoring. You may be terminal, you may recover, but you need a watchful eye over you.

Informed Consent A process of learning, usually from from your doctor, what treatment options are available to you (including none), with the benefits and risks of each, so you can make the final treatment decision yourself. Every human being of adult years and sound mind has a right to determine what shall be done with his own body. See Ch. 5.

Intubation A procedure used to provide air to lungs, or food to stomach. Several different kinds of intubation can be used. When intubated, you can't talk or breathe on our own. You are hooked up to a **Ventilator.** An LST. See Ch. 2.

Living Trust See **Trust.**

Living Will Same as **Health Care Directive.** See Ch. 2.

LSTs: Life-Sustaining Treatments Ways of prolonging your life, usually when you are near the end of your life. Your doctor can advise you of benefits and risks of your condition so you can decide what you want done, if anything. Benefits and risks of several LSTs are described in Ch. 2.

Natural Death Acts Between 1976 and 1992, all the states passed Natural Death Acts, which allow you to choose certain Life-Sustaining Treatments—through your Agent—even after you are unable to speak for yourself.

Pacemaker A device implanted in your chest to control abnormal heart rhythms. An LST. See Ch. 2.

Palliative Care Care which relieves symptoms without curing them, given to relieve suffering and control discomfort near end of life.

Patient Centered Decision Making A form of communicating with your physician that produces a statement of medical needs combined with your values, including Death with Dignity where it's legal. Similar to **Shared Decision Making.** See Ch. 5.

PEG: Percutaneous Endoscopic Gastronomy An LST. See Ch. 2.

Physician Assisted Dying Special state laws that provide for physician supervision of a patient's choice to die by his/her own hand. See **Death with Dignity**, also see Ch. 4.

POA: (Non-durable) **Power of Attorney** See Ch. 3 for comparison with **DPOA**.

POLST: Physician Orders for Life-Sustaining Treatment A signed physician's order for use in emergencies, and most states also require the patient's signature. Similar forms are called MOLST, MOST, POST. See Ch. 3.

Proxy (see **Agent, Attorney-in-Fact**) A general term for a person who acts for another, by relationship, appointment, or by custom.

PVS: Persistent Vegetative State A disorder of consciousness or brain damage where patients are unable to communicate or take care of themselves in any way.

Sanctity of Life A religious concept that life is a gift from God and only God can end it.

Shared Decision Making The goal of similarly named programs is to help patients make well-informed decisions that reflect their values and goals with their clinician. Similar to **Patient Centered Decision Making.** See Ch. 5.

Surgery An LST. See Ch. 2.

Terminal If your doctor declares you "terminal," he/she would not be surprised if you were to die within 6 months to a year. Often defined in state Natural Death Acts.

Trust (also Living Trust) A legal document providing for disposition of assets, liabilities and personal property upon one's death. Search Nolo Press for chart of comparison.

Ventilator A machine that helps a patient breathe. One type of **Intubation.** See Ch. 2.

VSED: Voluntary Stopping Eating and Drinking A legal form of taking your own life.

Will Legal document providing for disposition of your assets, liabilities and personal property after you die. Appoints a Personal Representative.

Withdrawing or Withholding Treatment A decision to provide either hospice or palliative care after patient's condition has progressed from acute to chronic condition.

Zone of Indistinction A special unit where PVS and similar patients are tended, their consciousness now indistinct. See Sharon R. Kaufman, *And a Time to Die*, pp. 273-317.

BIBLIOGRAPHY

This symbol (▶) indicates a focus on the rising costs of drugs, devices and procedures; and many ways to bring them into better balance with other developed countries.

Alpert, Richard (Ram Dass). *Still Here: Embracing Aging, Changing, and Dying.* New York: Riverhead Books, 2000.

Angell, Marcia. *The Truth About the Drug Companies.* New York: Random House, 2004.

Aries, Philippe. *The Hour of Our Death.* New York: Vintage Books, 1982.

Blank, Robert H. and Janna C. Merrick, eds. *End-of-Life Decision Making: A Cross-National Study.* Cambridge Massachusetts Institute of Technology Press, 2005.

▶**Brawley, Otis Webb with Paul Goldberg.** *How We Do Harm: A Doctor Breaks Ranks About Being Sick in America.* New York: St. Martin's Griffin 2011.

▶**Brill, Steven.** *America's Bitter Pill: Money Politics, Backroom Deals, and the Fight to Fix Our Broken Health Care System.* New York: Random House, 2015.

Brody, Jane. *Jane Brody's Guide to the Great Beyond: A Practical Primer to Help You and Your Loved Ones Prepare Medically, Legally, and Emotionally for the End of Life.* New York: Random House, 2009.

Buchwald, Art. *Too Soon to Say Goodbye.* New York: Random House, 2006.

Byock, Ira, Dying Well: Peace and Possibilities at the End of Life. New York: Riverhead Books, Berkeley Publishing Group, 1997.

Caplan, Arthur L.; James J. McCartney; and Dominic A. Sisti, eds. *The Case of Terri Schiavo: Ethic at the End of Life.* New York: Prometheus, 2006.

Carlson, Lisa. *I Died Laughing: Funeral Education with a Light Touch.* Hinesburg, VT: Upper Access, 2001.

Carney, Scott. *The Red Market: On the Trail of the World's Organ Brokers, Bone Thieves, Blood Farmers and Child Traffickers.* New York: William Morrow, 2011.

Carter, Jimmy. *The Virtues of Aging.* New York: Ballantine, 1998.

Chen, Pauline W. *Final Exam: A Surgeon's Reflections on Mortality.* New York: Vintage Books, 2008.

Chopra, Deepak. *Life After Death: The Burden of Proof.* New York: Harmony, 2006.

Cohen, Elizabeth. *The Empowered Patient: How to Get the Right Diagnosis, Buy the Cheapest Drugs, Beat Your Insurance Company and Get the Best Medical Care Every Time.* New York: Ballantine, 2010.

Colby, William H. *Unplugged: Reclaiming Our Right to Die in America.* New York: American Management Association, 2006.

———, *Long Goodbye: The Deaths of Nancy Cruzan.* Carlsbad, CA: Hay House, 2002.

Devettere, Raymond J. *Practical Decision Making in Health Care Ethics: Cases and Concept.* Washington, D.C.: Georgetown University Press, 2000.

Eisenberg, Jon B. *Using Terri: The Religious Right's Conspiracy to Take Away Our Rights.* HarperCollins, 2005.

Eisenberg, Mickey S., *Resuscitate! How Your Community Can Improve Survival from Sudden Cardiac Arrest.* Seattle: University of Washington Press, 2009.

Field, Marilyn J. *Approaching Death: Improving Care at the End of Life.* Washington, D.C.: National Academy Press, 1997.

Gawande, Atul. *Being Mortal: Medicine and What Matters in the End.* Edited by Christine K. Cassel. New York: Metropolitan, 2014.

———, *Checklist Manifesto: How to Get Things Right.* New York: Picador, 2011.

———, *Better: A Surgeon's Notes on Performance.* New York: Picador, 2006.

———, *Complications: A Surgeon's Notes on an Imperfect Science.* New York: Picador, 2002.

▶**Geyman, John.** *How Obamacare Is Unsustainable: Why We Need a Single-Payer Solution for All Americans.* Friday Harbor, WA: Copernicus Healthcare, 2015.

———, *The Corrosion of Medicine: Can the Profession Reclaim its Moral Legacy?* Monroe, ME: Common Courage, 2008.

▶**Goldhill, David.** *Catastrophic Care: How American Health Care Killed My Father—And How to Fix It.* New York: Alfred A. Knopf, 2013.

▶**Graedon, Joe and Teresa Graedon.** *Top Screwups Doctors Make and How to Avoid Them.* New York: Crown Archetype, 2011.

Groopman, Jerome and Pamela Hartzband. *Your Medical Mind: How to Decide What Is Right for You.* New York: Penguin, 2011.

Hahn, Thich Nhat. *No Death, No Fear: Comforting Wisdom for Life.* New York: Penguin Putnam, 2002.

Harris, Mark. *Grave Matters: A Journey Through the Modern Funeral Industry to a Natural Way of Burial.* New York: Scribner, 2008

▶**Herzlinger, Regina.** *Who Killed Health Care? America's $2 Trillion Dollar Medical Problem—and the Consumer-Driven Cure.* New York: McGraw-Hill, 2007.

Humphry, Derek. *Final Exit: The Practicalities of Self-Deliverance and Assisted Suicide for the Dying.* New York: Dell, (1991) 2002.

Jacoby, Susan. *Never Say Die: The Myth and Marketing of the New Old Age.* New York: Pantheon, 2011.

Jenkins, Margie. *You Only Die Once: Preparing for the End of Life with Grace and Gusto.* Brentwood, TN: Integrity, 2002

Johnson, Harriet McBryde, Too Late to Die Young: Nearly True Tales from a Life. *New York: Picador, 2005.*

Kaufman, Sharon R. *And a Time to Die: How American Hospitals Shape the End of Life.* Chicago: University of Chicago Press, 2006.

Kessler, David. *The Needs of the Dying.* New York: HarperCollins, 2000.

Kidder, Tracy. *Mountains Beyond Mountains: The Quest of Dr. Paul Farmer, A Man Who Would Cure the World.* New York: Random House, 2003.

Kiernan, Stephen P. *Last Rights: Rescuing the End of Life from the Medical System.* New York: St. Martin's Press, 2006.

Kübler-Ross, Elisabeth. *The Wheel of Life: A Memoir of Living and Dying.* New York: Touchstone, Simon & Schuster, 1998.

————, *On Death and Dying: What the Dying Have to Teach Doctors, Nurses, Clergy and Their Own Families*. New York: Touchstone, Simon & Schuster, 1997.

▶**Lazris, Andy.** *Curing Medicine: One Doctor's View of How our Health Care System Is Failing the Elderly and How to Fix It*. CreateSpace Independent Publishing Platform, 2014.

▶**Longman, Philip.** *Best Care Anywhere: Why VA Health Care Would Work Better for Everyone*. San Francisco: Barrett-Koehler, 2012.

▶**Lynn, Joanne.** *Sick to Death and Not Going to Take It Anymore! Reforming Health Care for the Last Years of Life*. Berkeley: University of California Press, 2004.

———— **and Joan Harrold.** *Handbook for Mortals: Guidance for People Facing Serious Illness*. New York: Oxford University Press, 1999.

MacGregor, Betsy. *In Awe of Being Human: A Doctor's Stories from the Edge of Life and Death*. Greenbank, WA: Abiding Nowhere Press, 2013.

▶**Mahar, Maggie.** *Money-Driven Medicine: The Real Reason Health Care Costs So Much*. New York: HarperCollins, 2006.

Markin, R.E. *The Affordable Funeral: Going in Style, Not in Debt*. Virginia Beach: F. Hooker, (1996) 2004.

▶**Mayer, Jane.** *Dark Money: the Hidden History of the Billionaires Behind the Rise of the Radical Right*. New York: Doubleday, 2016.

Mitford, Jessica. *The American Way of Death Revisited*. New York: Alfred A. Knopf, 1998.

Morris, Virginia. *Talking About Death*. Chapel Hill: Algonquin, 2001.

Nuland, Sherwin B. *The Art of Aging*. New York: Random House, 2007.

————, *How We Die: Reflections on Life's Final Chapter*. New York: Random House, 1995.

Pausch, Randy. *The Last Lecture (with Jeffrey Zaslow)*. New York: Hyperion, 2008.

▶**Potter, Wendell.** *Deadly Spin: An Insurance Company Insider Speaks Out on How Corporate PR Is Killing Health Care and Deceiving Americans.* New York: Bloomsbury, 2010.

▶**Potter, Wendell and Nick Penniman.** *Nation on the Take: How Big Money Corrupts Our Democracy.* New York: Bloomsbury, 2016.

President's Commission for the Study of Ethical Problems in Medicine and Biomedical and Behavioral Research. *Deciding to Forego Life-Sustaining Treatment: A Report on the Ethical, Medical and Legal Issues in Treatment Decisions.* New York: Concern for Dying, 1983.

President's Commission for the Study of Ethical Problems in Medicine and Biomedical and Behavioral Research. *Defining Death: A Report on the Medical, Legal and Ethical Issues in the Determination of Death.* Washington, D.C.: President's Commission for the Study of Ethical Problems in Medicine and Biomedical and Behavioral Research, 1981.

President's Council on Bioethics. *Controversies in the Determination of Death: a White Paper of the President's Council on Bioethics.* Washington, D.C.: President's Council on Bioethics, 2008.

President's Council on Bioethics. *Taking Care: Ethical Caregiving in Our Aging Society.* Washington, D.C.: President's Council on Bioethics, 2005.

Quill, Timothy F. *and Margaret P.* Batton, Physician-Assisted Dying: The Case for Palliative Care and Patient Choice. Baltimore: John Hopkins University Press, 2004.

Quinlan, Joseph and Julia Quinlan with Phyllis Battelle. *Karen Ann: The Quinlans Tell Their Story.* New York: Bantam, 1977.

▶**Reid, T.R.** *The Healing of America: A Global Quest for Better, Cheaper, and Fairer Health Care.* New York: Penguin, 2009.

Schiavo, Michael with Michael Hirsh. *Terri, the Truth.* New York: Penguin, 2006.

Shaw, Eva. *What to Do When a Loved One Dies: A Practical and Compassionate Guide to Dealing with Death on Life's Terms.* Irvine: Dickens Press 1994.

Simpson, Jan. *Don't Give Up on Me! Supporting Aging Parents Successfully.* Concord, MA: Circle of Life Partners, 2010.

▶**Smith, Jeremy N.** *Epic Measures: One Doctor. Seven Billion Patients.* New York: HarperCollins, 2015.

Sweet, Victoria. *God's Hotel: a Doctor, a Hospital, and a Pilgrimage to the Heart of Medicine.* New York: Riverhead Books, (2012) 2013.

Terkel, Studs. *Will the Circle Be Unbroken? Reflections on Death, Rebirth, and Hunger for a Faith.* New York: Ballantine, 2001.

Terman, Stanley A. with Ronald Baker Miller and Michael S. Evans. *The Best Way to Say Goodbye: A Legal Peaceful Choice at the End of Life.* Carlsbad: Life Transitions, 2007.

Thornhill, Matt and John Martin. *Boomer Consumer: Ten New Rules for Marketing to America's Largest, Wealthiest and Most Influential Group.* Great Falls, VA: Linx, 2007.

Timmermans, Stefan. *The Sudden Death and the Myth of CPR.* Philadelphia: Temple University Press, 1999.

Torrey, Trisha. *You Bet Your Life! The 10 Mistakes Every Patient Makes: How to Fix Them to Get the Health Care You Deserve.* Minneapolis: Langdon Street Press, 2010.

Trowbridge, David Daiku. *Enso House: Caring for Each Other at the End of Life.* Greenbank, WA: Abiding Nowhere Press, 2013.

Verghese, Abraham. *Cutting for Stone: A Novel.* New York: Vintage, 2010.

Wanzer, Sydney and Joseph Glenmullen. *To Die Well: Your Right to Comfort, Calm, and Choice in the Last Days of Life.* Philadelphia: DaCapo, 2007.

Warner, Jan and Jan Collins. *Next Steps: A Practical Guide to Planning for the Best Half of Your Life.* Fresno: Quill Driver, 2009.

▶**Welch, H. Gilbert.** *Less Medicine, More Health.* Boston: Beacon Press, 2015.

Wen, Leana and Joshua Kosowsky. *When Doctors Don't Listen: How to Avoid Misdiagnosis and Unnecessary Tests.* New York: St. Martin's, 2012.

INDEX

ABOUT THE AUTHOR

As a child, my parents committed me to one-half hour piano practice before breakfast every school morning. My two brothers and I did a weekly cycle to see who had to get up first. Choice was limited but discipline was not. Having choice within boundaries shaped my personal discipline through most of my life.

Education was highly valued, even though providing it wasn't easy during the 1940s. But we worked it out—I was expected to earn part of my way. I went to Beloit College, the University of Wisconsin, Madison, and received a BS degree in business from University of California, Berkeley. Eventually, University of Southern California awarded me an MBA in 1948. I was one of only two women who received that degree that year. I went on to teach Management Development for Women at UCLA Extension, and co-authored my first book with Rosalind Loring, *Breakthrough: Women Into Management*. This led to invitations for articles in several management books and journals, and speaking engagements. Giving speeches was not my style—I stimulated talk-discussions instead. This helped address anger released in previously all-male departments, whether in business organizations, professional groups or universities. Glass ceilings still exist but expectations have shifted, though uneasily.

Of course, none of this hard-won wisdom sells unless we sprinkle in humor to ease transitions in corporate life, a goal of my last book *Keeping Your Cool Under Fire: Communicating Non-Defensively,* 1980. Now that I'm turning 90, I started thinking about how to die well, so I got to work on *Take Care of Dying—Get On with Living: End-of-Life Planning that Works*, 2016. I trust it works as well for you as it has for me.

66758645R00096

Made in the USA
Lexington, KY
25 August 2017